Reflections on a Life

Reflections on a Life

Norbert Elias

Includes 'Biographical Interview with Norbert Elias'
by A. J. Heerma van Voss and A. van Stolk

Translated by Edmund Jephcott

Polity Press

This translation © 1994 Polity Press

Published in German as *Norbert Elias über sich selbst*, © 1990 Norbert Elias Stichting.

Originally published in Dutch as *De geschiedenis van Norbert Elias*, 1987; interview Norbert Elias © A. J. Heerma van Voss and A. van Stolk.

First published in 1994 by Polity Press in association with Blackwell Publishers.

Editorial office:
Polity Press
65 Bridge Street
Cambridge CB2 1UR, UK

Marketing and production:
Blackwell Publishers
108 Cowley Road
Oxford OX4 1JF, UK

238 Main Street
Cambridge, MA 02142, USA

ISBN 0 7456 1276 8
ISBN 0 7456 1383 7 (pbk)

A CIP catalogue record for this book is available from the British Library and the Library of Congress.

Typeset in 11 on 13 pt Sabon Symposia by Apex Products, Singapore
Printed in Great Britain by T. J. Press, Padstow, Cornwall

This book is printed on acid-free paper

Contents

—●◆—

Acknowledgements   vii

Biographical Interview with Norbert Elias   1
A. J. Heerma van Voss and A. van Stolk

Notes on a Lifetime   81
Norbert Elias

Chronology   155
Select Bibliography   157
Index   159

Acknowledgements

The 'Biographical interview with Norbert Elias' as it appears in this edition makes extensive use of the original English transcript kindly made available by Arend-Jan Heerma van Voss and Bram van Stolk, edited as in the Dutch edition, *De geschiedenis van Norbert Elias* (Meulenhoff, Amsterdam, 1987). 'Notes on a lifetime' was first published in *Macht und Zivilisation. Materialien zu Norbert Elias' Zivilisationstheorie 2*, ed. Peter Gleichmann, Johan Goudsblom and Hermann Korte (Suhrkamp, Frankfurt, 1984), pp. 9–82. It has been translated from the German edition of this book, *Norbert Elias über sich selbst* (Suhrkamp, Frankfurt, 1990).

Biographical Interview with Norbert Elias

A. J. Heerma van Voss and
A. van Stolk

Norbert Elias has often been interviewed about his thought, but seldom about his life – a subject that concerns him much less. His own *Notizen zum Lebenslauf* ('Notes on a lifetime', reprinted in this volume) likewise deal mainly with his intellectual development. Alfred Weber and Karl Mannheim, sociologists from the time of the Weimar Republic, appear in the notes as the principal figures in a narrative which is more an essay than an autobiography; the first section is entitled 'What learning taught me'.

What experience taught Norbert Elias he tells us in seven conversations we had with him in 1984, which together account for about twenty hours of tape recordings. Three of these conversations were held in Bielefeld, in his study in the Zentrum für interdisziplinäre Forschung (ZiF), four in his apartment in south Amsterdam.

The ZiF, attached to the university, is in the southern outskirts of Bielefeld, on the edge of the Teutoburger Wald. It is a modern complex, very quiet, a place where scholars from various disciplines live and work. In Elias's apartment the keynote was set by printed and handwritten paper: books, journals, manuscripts, files, letters, newspapers. He began his normal working day, seven days a week, at 11 a.m.; at 2 p.m. his male or female assistant arrived, an undergraduate or research student, and worked with him until ten at night. Elias dictated texts, corrected the different versions and dealt with his correspondence. Sometimes the assistant had difficulty keeping up, sometimes there were long pauses. The work was interrupted only by a walk in the forest and by the evening meal – always at the Greek restaurant in the nearby university building.

In Amsterdam a similar routine was followed, with the Vondelpark standing in for the Teutoburger Wald and a pizzeria for the Greek restaurant. The house there was more inviting, especially since the collection of African art and the library had arrived from Leicester – Elias had left Leicester years before, but his furniture and household effects were kept there for a long time.

Elias did not lead the life of an old man: even when he was not working, he was active, with a certain compulsive urgency. He wrote poems, most of which have by now been published, followed world events through the *Herald Tribune* and the BBC News; he swam, travelled and took an interest in the ups and downs in his friends' lives. Only latterly, as a concession to his advancing years, did he have to limit the range of these activities.

Once he had been won over to the plan of an extensive biographical interview, he sometimes showed more stamina than his interviewers, whose combined ages were less than his. Any tiredness was shown by a heightened abstractness, not by getting bogged down in concrete details.

The conversations were conducted in English. Elias weighed his words, articulating them emphatically, with an expressive delivery.

'My memory is still very good,' he said, 'although I have lived so long. Perhaps my desire to remember the past has grown stronger in recent years. Pictures and faces rise up from the dim past. I even remember some names. But a great part of my life has been completely taken up with my work.'

We begin in Breslau, which for several decades has been a part of Poland and is now called Wrocław.

Do you remember any time in your life when you were not already working?

... No.

When did you start working, at what age? At school?

At primary school, yes. I had all the childhood illnesses one could possibly have. My parents thought me too delicate to start in the first form – which in those days was called the eighth, counting backwards. I only remember very vividly that they hired the class teacher, who normally taught the children at school. That's when I started working.

You mean, at six or seven.

Yes, probably – I don't know exactly when. I started reading very early, browsing in all kinds of books. I must have been about six or seven.

Do you have the feeling that you chose it yourself – the importance of work?

... I don't think one can ever say one chooses things. I had a very hard-working father, and an absolutely non-working mother. Although – that's not quite right. She worked, of course, when we had guests. She worked very hard preparing for parties. She was the nicest mother you could think of, very jolly, happy, outgoing.

You were born on 22 June 1897, in Breslau. How long did you live there?

I lived there until I became a soldier – that is to say until 1915. I went straight from school into the army. When the war was over, I went back home.

That means that you spent your first eighteen years in Breslau. Can you give us any idea what kind of a place it was?

Yes... We lived in a two-storey house, with apartments of seven or eight rooms, I think, or maybe six. I've forgotten. A corner house; the front windows and the front door faced the former city moat which, as in other German towns, had been turned into a little waterway. The old fortifications had become a promenade, for walking, where there were benches, children playing, plenty of trees. So we had a very pleasant view from the front, and in winter – every winter, as far as I remember – the water was frozen solid, and people were skating. You could look on this very vivid picture, and sometimes I went out skating myself.

So out to the front was this very pleasant landscape, and the other windows looked out on to a side-street, part of a rather poor neighbourhood. So I grew up from an early age in, I wouldn't say genteel surroundings, but very middle-class ones, for my parents naturally had to show off their status as quite well-off people. So they had to live in a presentable neighbourhood, which at the same time, just round the corner, was a rather poor one.

I shall never forget the children of the caretaker of the house, who lived in the cellar. You went down some stairs to the small basement flat, where the children lived that I sometimes played with: a girl and a boy who ran about in summer without shoes or socks. That is very vivid in my memory, that kind of poverty – though they were not as poor as all that. I mean, as a caretaker he was probably paid very little, but they had the flat for nothing, in the basement, with a window and a small front garden.

Were they rich people who went walking on the promenade?

No, they were all kinds of people. I should say that it wasn't the best middle-class area in Breslau. But it was quite respectable, partly because the rooms were very big, at least the drawing rooms, where you held social gatherings or received visitors. We had an extra salon that was only used for visitors, one of those big drawing rooms where friends of my mother could gather for tea or coffee.

So the people on the promenade were mixed. Many of the children were taken out for walks there by their *Kinderfräulein* [nursemaid], and I often went walking there too, playing with children and rolling my hoop.

Was it a rich city?

Yes, Breslau was wealthy, with a very prosperous agricultural area around it – the great Silesian estate owners, mostly aristo-crats. The Silesian Catholic aristocracy was all around, and the city itself was old, with a splendid Renaissance Rathaus and an old Jesuit university. It was an area steeped in old culture.

But one which had earlier belonged to Poland?

In the Middle Ages, yes. Or rather, things were not so fixed. Silesia belonged to a Polish dynasty, partly Germanized. Then it became part of Austria, until Frederick the Great conquered it for Prussia. In the seventeenth century, when much of Germany was devastated by war, Breslau was one of the few towns able to buy its immunity from the marauders. And in this period the main German literature was written in Breslau. When the rest of the country was dreadfully ravaged by the roving armies, the Swedes, the imperial troops and so on, Breslau was relatively unscathed. So it has a long tradition.

How many inhabitants did it have around the turn of the century?

When I was there, I think it had about 500,000.

Was it a beautiful city?

In parts, in the centre. A very fine Rathaus, on the main square called the 'Ring'. It was surrounded by big houses, one of which belonged to my father; a commercial building that went through to the next street. It was really two houses. It was right in the centre. I still remember the number – Ring 16.

That's where my father had his business. He was in textiles, manufacturing, as were many Jews. He had probably started about 1880 or 1885 and was carried along by the prosperity which had come after 1870. It was a kind of factory, but with relatively few machines, mainly people working by hand. About thirty people, including tailors, making clothes for the wholesale trade.

To come back to Breslau – did it feel like a German city?

Completely German – completely. No Polish element. If you went further down in Silesia, you came to an area where there was a mixture – for example, what you read about now in the paper as Katowice – that was German. In upper Silesia you had a bit of mixed population. But Breslau was completely German – there were no Poles there. Or the Poles who were there were completely Germanized. I never heard a Polish word there.

Had your family lived in Breslau for several generations? Where did your parents come from?

They were part of the migratory movements of Jews. That is to say, my father came from a little town in what was then a German province. It is now called Poznan and was then called Posen. A little town that was probably populated mainly by Jews, but there he already went to the German grammar school.

I think he deeply regretted not having been able to go to university, because his family did not have enough money. That's why it was important to him to pass on that ambition to his son. He would have liked to study medicine, and so I enrolled for medicine partly for his sake. I was the only son, after all – their only child. So he transferred everything he had not been able to achieve to me.

Was your father German?

Oh yes, very much – very Prussian. He thought of himself as German and nothing else. His parents' and grandparents' portraits hung in our house, so that their loss affects me very much. They were also German, though from somewhat further east. My mother's parents were German, too, but she could still remember their own parents having lived in Poland.

Did Breslau have a rich cultural life? Was it a lively town?

A lively town? Certainly. It had a rich cultural life. But I knew it mostly through good Jewish society. I mean, they formed a closely knit kind of bourgeoisie, where it was taken for granted that every winter one went to the 'orchestral concerts', as they were called. My mother had a reserved seat for them every winter, and in the Lobe Theatre. It was the done thing.

I myself must have felt I wanted to get away from it as soon as I could.

Why?

I ... can't really call that back now. In my present-day words I would say it was too bourgeois for me; but I should not have expressed it like that at the time. I mean, my mother had a whole circle of woman friends, from the same stratum, many wealthier than we were, who came every week. Then there were my aunts – it was not my cup of tea. But I wouldn't have called it 'bourgeois', because I was not politically minded at all.

'Bourgeois' can also have an emotional meaning. Was that world too narrow for you?

I had slightly the feeling that it was also below my level, below my intellectual level.

When did you get that feeling?

It must have been very early. I think I recognized very early that what they were saying was *Gewäsch* [prattle] – not very profound.

And your father's circle?

My father had no circle. To begin with, he concentrated entirely on his work. He then gave up his business very early, at fifty. He had enough money, and from then on did honorary things. I can only remember one friend of his, a lawyer. All his social relations were mediated by my mother.

Did he not have the time for it?

I think he had a very high degree of sublimation, into work. And when he gave up the business, he still had houses to administer, apart from his honorary duties. He was very devoted to that, and to his family, of course – my mother and me.

You were an only child?

An only child, yes... I mean, I now sometimes find the similarity of my sitting in a chair and just thinking, and what I see my father doing: sitting there and just thinking something out. I remember that very vividly – his image, just sitting there. As a child I must sometimes have puzzled over what he was actually doing. When I was very little I may not have understood.

Did he look out of the window?

No. He was just sitting there, thinking.... Well, I mean, he may have looked out of the window, that I cannot say, but that is not the gesture I remember. As I remember him, he was sitting on the sofa and thinking things out or being absorbed in something.

Do you know what he thought about?

No – probably about his business. He never talked very much about his affairs. He certainly kept his financial affairs entirely to himself. That must have been a very strong tradition.

Did he tell you about other things on his mind?

One thing I remember is a very remarkable attempt he made to 'enlighten' me, *aufklären*, on sexual matters. One can hardly imagine that today. He obviously felt that it was his duty. I still remember that it was awkward. It was not something he liked doing, but he felt he had to do it. Somehow he was an enormously dutiful person.

Was he lonely?

I do not think he was lonely because my parents had a very good marriage. It was, in a way, the old-fashioned type of marriage – what you call 'harmonious inequality'. A model of harmonious inequality: he took all the decisions, but that was what she wanted. My mother was quite unable to cope with financial affairs; nor did she need to. On the other hand, she was the one who took all social matters in hand. When there was a visit to be made, she pushed him out, saying: 'Let's go.' No, I don't think he was lonely.

Did you ever ask your parents why you were an only child?

No such questions would be discussed.

And you were not curious?

One did not talk about sexual matters – except that attempt to enlighten me.

Did you never regret not having any brothers or sisters?

Not that I recollect. But I do still have a very strong feeling that it is not good for children to grow up as I did, and that must mean that I wanted brothers and sisters – even if perhaps unconsciously. But of course there were always the governesses.

So you had some company. Do you remember them?

Yes, but they are dim figures. And there were many of them. From very early days, a nanny, and then a governess who was very nice. The last one was when I was eleven or twelve. Then I got a very educated lady, who came from a good family, now impoverished.

Norbert Elias with his mother (left) and a nanny, about 1906

When you were young, did you feel part of a bigger whole?
We were a fairly large family group when I was a child:
father, mother, cook, governess and I. That was the group to
which I belonged. Then there were aunts and my grandmother
– yes, of course, my mother's parents were also part of it.
We went to see them almost every day; they lived in the same

neighbourhood. That's why we lived there – so that my mother could easily visit my grandparents. So that was the group, an extended family.

And did you feel yourself to be part of the Jewish community, or of the city as a whole?

Well, that – forgive me for saying so – would give me a level of consciousness that I certainly did not have. It may have been so, but not with that level of consciousness.

Of course, I belonged to Breslau, that was taken for granted. And the country was taken for granted as well. I knew that the Kaiser existed, but he was something very dim and remote... I knew that I was a German and a Jew. Yes, of course, we went to the synagogue once a year or so, on big festival days. So I must have known that I was a Jew, and I knew that I was a German. It was all on an unreflecting level, as far as I can see. I would falsify it if I said yes to your question.

You can remember it, but you cannot remember thinking about it.

Quite. That was how the world was. It was all taken absolutely for granted. It was much later that I started to ask questions.

What was the stronger feeling – being a Jew or being a German?

Forgive me for saying so, but that is an entirely wrong question.

Why?

Because the two things were not competing in any way. Of course I was both, as one would say existentially, in a completely unreflecting way.

And you never thought about being one thing more than the other?

No. From your question I actually see how much more explicit all that has become than it was when I was young.

Did you ever think about it when you were a child?

I doubt it.

Did you ever think about the fact that there were other people who were Germans and not Jews, and others who were Jews and not Germans?

Of course I knew when I was very little, when I played with the caretaker's children, that they were poorer and were not Jews. But that was what the world was like. It seems to me that maybe social science has made us much more given to explicate such things than at the time when there was no social science.

So you never had any idea of belonging to two different nationalities, or anything like that?

No, not at all. There was no question that one was a German. As I said, my father was very Prussian. He had the same moustache as the Emperor, and he had a bandage he put on it to make the points stand up. He was a very good person, quite without false hardness, but he certainly knew himself to be a Prussian and a German, and so it was self-evident to me too.

Did the Jews in Breslau consider themselves Germans like other Germans, or did they sometimes consider themselves better Germans than the others?

They considered themselves Germans, but as I see it now, in a taken-for-granted way. But they had a real contempt for anti-Semites. Their defence mechanism was that those people were not worth talking about. That is as I recollect the attitude. It was not a question for them whether they were Germans – they *were* Germans. But those who said they were not were pushed back in their own minds as uncivilized, not to be taken seriously.

Were there many people who talked about anti-Semitism?

There was not a lot of talk about it, but I was conscious of it. There was not really much need to take notice of it. It was not very obtrusive, but when it was in the papers, Jews were presented as uncivilized, uneducated people.

Were they really like that?

No, far from it. From my own theory, I think it must have been a particularly annoying quality of Jews that they did not recognize their own inferiority.

How do you mean that?

Well, if you take the point of view of a person who has, as a matter of course, a contempt for Jews as an inferior group, it is particularly annoying that these people do not seem to know that they are inferior. And that is indeed how it was. One had no such feeling. In fact, one had a contempt for those who said Jews were inferior.

Was there any feeling among Jews of not being inferior, but in fact superior?

That may also have been the case. I cannot say from memory: superior to *whom*. Certainly superior to anti-Semites, but certainly not superior to the Emperor, or to the German bureaucracy, who were obviously people of higher standing.

Do you remember any anti-Semitism directed towards yourself?

Yes; for example, there was an incident at grammar school, when I was 15 or 16. We talked in class about our plans for a career. I said I wanted to be a professor at the university, and a classmate interjected, '*That* career was cut off for you at birth.' There was a lot of laughter, from the teacher and, of course, the whole class. And it wasn't really meant maliciously, it was a very astute remark. It wounded me so much because I had probably never realized that under the Emperor such a career was practically closed to Jews.

And then... I have a vague recollection of street urchins, *Gassenjungen* as we called them, chanting 'Judenjunge, Judenjunge' ['Jewboy, jewboy'] after me when I went out with my governess. I remember something like that, probably when I was five or six. But we knew they were just urchins. There were no Jewish factory workers, at least, not as far as I remember. I see Jews as a solid middle-class group – with the poor Jews, the immigrants from the east, who spoke Yiddish. But even they were not factory workers.

Were the wealthier and better educated Germans really less anti-Semitic?

No, no, I have only given you what I believe was the perspective of my childhood. Today I regard that as self-deception, an illusion. I mean the anti-Semitism of the upper classes was repressed. If it happened that someone from a conservative, good family made anti-Semitic remarks, it was dismissed as an exception. Take the Emperor: there was one Jew, a banker, who was occasionally invited to court. You could see from that that the Emperor was not anti-Semitic.

It was, of course, a form of self-defence. If the Jews had realized the degree to which anti-Semitism pervaded the whole of the German middle and upper classes, it would have taken away much of their own security.

They put their trust in the more educated people, which was rather naive.

Not so naive under the Emperor, because although there was a lot of anti-Semitism, and even the court preacher, Stoecker, was head of an anti-Semitic party, Germany was really what was called a *Rechtsstaat*, a constitutional state, which meant that if a Jew had to go to court and had a dispute with a gentile, he could be sure that justice would be done. And it was the state in which Jews could seek prosperity and standing.

But there must have been some collective memory that all that was a recent affair.

It was all a straight line of social ascent. I mean, my grandparents were probably better off than their parents, and my parents were better off than theirs. A rising line. What happened before, my great-grandparents in the ghetto, was in the distant past.

Were there no tales of pogroms?

In barbarian Russia, perhaps, but in Germany such things did not happen. Under the Emperor – impossible!

It is quite incredible, if you consider that there was a rising wave of anti-Semitism from the end of the nineteenth century. But that was the position: it cannot happen in Germany. And it could not happen under the Emperor.

You felt safe in Breslau?

Completely. It sounds incredible now, but yes, that is so. The Jewish community must have been blind, but blinded partly because they were prosperous.

It was really like the ancien régime. One could not imagine that the world would ever be different. And I also remember that, as in the ancien régime, some people felt that life was really a little boring. I vaguely remember that one writer in 1910 or 1911 committed suicide, and I seem to remember that some people made comments about life having become too uninteresting for him; it was boring. That feeling supplemented what I said about security: one could not imagine that anything new would ever happen.

With my better knowledge now, I know that some conservative leaders of that time were extremely frightened because the Social Democrats were getting more and more votes in the elections. They were aware that the 'red tide', *die rote Flut*, as they called it, was coming closer. But in the world in which I lived... no, I never heard the rumbling of the approaching thunderstorm.

For me the world only changed with the war. I still cannot really quite understand how I coped with this situation; the change from the complete security of my family to the complete insecurity of the army. Suddenly my parents were no longer there.

Was the security of your family complete?

Yes. Memories are, of course, deceptive, but as far as I remember it this was a secure world. I knew that my father would do anything for me, and my mother, too. If I was ill – and I was very frequently ill as a child – every care was taken; I felt completely protected. I always think that the staying power I had later, when I wrote my books and no one took any notice of them, was due to the very great security that I enjoyed as a child.

Perhaps I could express it in the following manner; just as astronomers have discovered that the whole universe is full of the radiation noise from the Big Bang, so people carry with them a background feeling about their existence that stems from their early days in their family. I have a background feeling of very great security, the feeling that fundamentally things will turn out all right, and I ascribe that to the enormous emotional security I had in the affection of my parents as an only child.

I knew from very early days what I wanted: I wanted to go to the university, I wanted to teach and I wanted to do research. I knew that from very early on and have pursued it, although it sometimes seemed impossible.

And you also knew you would be successful?

Yes. I actually wrote a very early poem about it. Well, there was an either/or situation: either I will be a great success, or

I will go under. Of course, I did not have absolute certainty, but rather great confidence that my work would eventually gain recognition as a useful contribution to the knowledge of mankind.

Wasn't that confidence shaken by the many illnesses you had in childhood?

No. When I was ill the whole of family life revolved around me.

But weren't you afraid?

I can still see my mother before me, sitting anxiously by my bed. I can't really remember any fear of death, although it must have been there. But all that – sexuality and death – was completely hidden behind the scenes. My parents were both very good people, and I knew I could rely on them absolutely – not in so many words, but as a feeling.

Have you ever regretted that that whole world changed?

No, never. As I grew older, I knew I could not live in that world. How can I explain it? It was not my world.

Then the war changed everything. When I came back, it was no longer my world.

Breslau was no longer the same?

No. For I had also changed myself. I changed during the war.

I still remember the day war broke out very clearly. We were on holiday in Scheveningen or Ostend, I cannot recollect which, and there, in August 1914, we caught the last train that could take us back to Germany. It was completely crowded with German families, withdrawing from the Netherlands or Belgium.

In that overcrowded train I made the acquaintance of a person whom I can only remember very dimly – we were standing in the corridor because the compartments were crowded. With him I discussed the latest edition of one of the avant-garde magazines of the time, *Der Sturm*, which was already printing woodcuts by Kokoschka and people like him. They were somehow leftist, but I was not committed to the left; but of course I was interested in this artistic movement, particularly in Expressionist poetry.

We had a long, intense discussion. Because I was so unpolitical, this person tried to explain some things from the magazine to me, so the many hours of the journey flew by. It may perhaps disappoint you, but I had no feeling about the war. I had no idea that it would be the end of the world I had known.

One was completely in the dark: it was war, but one couldn't connect that to anything, one had not had it before. I think it is always terrible that people reconstruct things afterwards as if they had a clear idea of what was to come. But I had no clear idea of that, not at all. In fact, I was anxious, and my parents were anxious, because I had to get back to school on time. That was why it was so important for us not to miss the train,

So that crowded train was my first war experience. Maybe others were talking about people being shot and wounded – I do not know. But nothing of that was on my mind. It was something very far off, battles, cannons. I mean, I lived in a completely unmilitary household. And then I did indeed go back to school.

You were just seventeen then, but did you have any idea about the reasons for the war? Did you have any feelings about your country, about Germany being attacked and having enemies?

Not that I can recollect. I do not think I was terribly interested.

Did you not have a feeling of righteousness – did you feel nationalistic?

Well, I hated the idea of the Kaiser, from a very young age.

Why?

The idea was abhorrent to me, that I would have to kowtow to this man, for whom I had no great respect, if he came along – that was the image I had. That there was someone who could demand subservience from me – I hated that idea.

Was that a widespread thought, or something personal?

That I cannot say. I know... my classmates must have felt it too, probably my Jewish classmates in particular. I remember that our headmaster was invited to the Kaiser's yacht and that he gave an account of it, and we found all that rather ridiculous. No, although it was taken for granted that we were Germans, there was no identification with the Kaiser.

Johannes-Gymnasium in Breslau

That surprises me.

It was a strong feeling in me from very early on. But there was also literature in that direction. A science fiction novel of that time, *Auf zwei Planeten* ['On two planets'] by Kurt Lasswitz, describes war between the Martians and Earth people. The Martians had a big magnet on an airship, and I think one of the last scenes in the book, which is very much in my memory, shows the Kaiser having a big parade, marching up all his troops somewhere, and then there came this big magnet from the Martians, and all the metal things from the soldiers flew up to the magnet. I quite liked the idea. I liked the idea of the Emperor looking ridiculous.

Weren't you proud of your country?

I never was a patriot. The Jews have sometimes been reproached with that – not being patriotic. My father was a patriot in a way, but I was completely against it.

In my view that was one of the reasons for anti-Semitism. The German *Bürger*, the bourgeoisie, unanimously welcomed the war. Almost all the younger members of the higher Jewish middle class were more or less to the left or at least liberal, while the great majority of the German middle class was to the right.

Yet you still felt you were a German.

Oh yes, completely, but I did not share the enthusiasm for the war. I always thought that the Kaiser and his whole circle were terrible people.

Opposition was in the air at that time. It did not take a political form with me, but I remember that in 1913 there was a big centenary celebration of the victory over Napoleon. Breslau built a festival hall for the occasion, where a festival performance by Gerhart Hauptmann was put on. Now Hauptmann was slightly leftist – not at all revolutionary or anything of that kind – but because he was the author the Kaiser refused to come to Breslau and open the festival hall. There was a great scandal, and we all found that ridiculous. So there was really a considerable atmosphere of antagonism in the air. I mean, that was a year before the war. So he was generally seen as a ridiculous person.

If you were never a patriot, what was your feeling about Germany without the Kaiser?

I never thought about the possibility. One could not imagine any other Germany. That does not mean one agreed with it.

All the same, I loved Germany very much. I was steeped in German *Kultur*. That is an old German problem, and very difficult to make clear: that one can identify oneself strongly with the German cultural tradition – as I still do – without therefore being, let's not say a patriot, but a nationalist.

I was never a nationalist. The nationalists in Germany were, of course, anti-Semites by that time.

But through identifying with the German cultural tradition, could you not be proud of being a German?

I cannot put it into those words. I am proud of being in that tradition. I identified very much with German classicism – Goethe, Schiller, Kant: they were the great men in my life. My first printed essay was full of allusions to them.

Were you, to use your own terms, a member of the established or an outsider in Germany?

Objectively speaking, of course an outsider.

And emotionally speaking?

I was never for the war, never for the Kaiser – secretly, I was always against all that. I probably never talked about it, but from my feelings, without reflection, that was certain: it is not my world, I have nothing to do with it. That feeling was very strong in me. That might be called the outsider position, although I could not have expressed it like that at the time. On the other hand, there was an element of self-protection in all that... The funny side of the situation was that Jewish society saw itself particularly as a carrier of German culture. And it was true in a way that without the patronage of Jewish society the orchestral concerts, the Lobe Theatre and all the other theatres could not have maintained themselves. It was a very odd situation. Politically the Jews were outsiders, yet at the same time they were carriers of German cultural life.

You loved Germany. Was there a time when you went out wandering in the countryside, as one reads the young people of that time did?

Yes, I had an enormous admiration for the German landscape. Even much later, in my early twenties, I had a very intimate knowledge of all the cathedrals – Bamberg, for example. I knew all the buildings by heart, all the styles. And actually there was a Jewish youth movement that was completely orientated towards these German things.

We'd like to ask some questions about other countries in Europe at that time. What did you know and what was your feeling about England, for example?

For some reason unknown to me, from very early days I had an emotional preference for France, not for England. Even at school I subscribed to the *Revue Française* – a journal for German schools, I think – to improve my French. I even wrote an essay for it, in a competition in which you could win a trip to France, but I did not get the prize. England I didn't like.

And Russia?

Nothing, absolutely nothing. The Tsar and the Cossacks, barbarous. The barbarous east – that was all beyond the pale. 'Polish Jew' was almost a term of abuse.

Poland, of course, was a Russian protectorate at that time?

That may be – but it existed all the same. In Silesia, at any rate, you grew up with the implicit prejudice that 'Polacken' were people of an inferior kind.

And countries like Romania and Bulgaria?

Beyond the pale. The Balkans were part of the Orient. At that time the Orient started there. Perhaps we do not realize that the scope of the term has shifted: the Balkan question was the oriental question.

As a German, did you feel part of the west?

That was not the expression at that time. At that time there was Orient and Occident; in *The Civilizing Process* I still use the word 'occidental'.

But there was a feeling about Western Europe and Central Europe?

Mitteleuropa, certainly – but that was Europe, it was the Occident, *das Abendland*. Whereas the Balkans were already the *Morgenland*, the east, oriental, and so on. Of course, one grew up with a lot of implicit ethnic biases, one of which was that the Orient was a world of lower cultural value – culture was always the main principle.

Did you understand anything about the reasons why Germany went to war with other occidental countries?

First of all, I do not think we were told that Germany went to war. We were told that Germany was attacked.

Which country did you see as the main enemy?

... I have no recollection – I probably did not think in those bellicose terms. I may be quite wrong, but I have no recollection of having had a bad feeling about enemies. The Russians were barbarians, that was quite clear, and we did not want the Cossacks to come to Breslau.

I did not identify with Germany in a military way; I had nothing to do with that. Even in the army I was never a nationalist or patriot – I just went into the *Wurstmaschine*, the sausage machine because I had to.

Do you remember any expressions of war fever around you, in 1914?

No, when the war started I was still at school. As far as I can recollect, I do not think there was much enthusiasm. I only know it from literature.

And the literature says there was great enthusiasm and they all thought they would win.

Yes. In a lecture I once quoted from a letter of a young student, who wrote to the effect that: 'You can be proud, for you will be able to say that you have lived in a great time – we will win, there is no doubt about it,' and so on; and two days later he was dead. It was a terrible thing, this slaughter of young people, the best volunteers, in the first days of the war, and all because of a complete military misjudgement on the part of the French as well as the German general staff.

On both sides the generals followed the dictates of their mentalities. The French as well as the Germans planned for a quick victory by offensive, so that they collided together in the first days of the war at enormous cost of life, and then the war got bogged down. The firepower of the defensive guns was so superior that it was impossible to break through. A non-military person like H. G. Wells had foreseen it, but the experts had not.

I still feel to this day that after wars one should make clearer the wrong judgements the mentality of the generals led to. Men like Ludendorff and Hindenburg lead their people; then they lose the war; the people have to bear the consequences and the leaders live on as if it had not been their fault. Hindenburg, Hitler, the Kaiser – they all made the biggest mistakes, and everyone can recognize them as such. And the worst thing that can happen to them is suicide. And the people are left in a mess. That could happen again today.

Do you mean that such leaders are stupid, or are you saying that you hate them?

No, no. I want to tell them that they are stupid. They wear professional blinkers, and in my own field I dislike and despise people who allow their own wishes to obscure the realities of the situation. And these military people wished for a quick attack, that was in their blood. So they planned accordingly, although the reality could have shown them they could not win.

But you don't hate them?

It is not a question of hatred. It is a question of... I still have the feeling that people in my position, by presenting the facts in a way everyone can understand, could prevent a good many of the mistakes of today.

That is a high ambition.

Oh, I know that I have not achieved it. But that, I think, is not just an ambition for myself; I am convinced that it is the task of sociology.

Of course, the situation today is very different, because that kind of illusion has been driven out by the two world wars. What one has to tell people more clearly is that Russia and America, against the wishes of their leaders, may be driven into a situation where they feel they must start an atomic war. That is to say, one has to lay bare the constraints to which they are exposed – what I have called the double-bind. This is not a matter of rational decisions. One can say exactly that one side fears being driven into a corner, and therefore starts a nuclear war, against its own will.

I personally believe – and this is the 'high ambition' you just spoke about – that a realistic analysis of interstate relationships could help to lessen the likelihood of an atomic war. It is not a personal ambition; I am too old, but it is something which ought to be done. It is a bit like the natural sciences: you cannot prevent lightning from striking, or an epidemic, without knowing the cause for them: but if you know the cause, you can prevent both.

Has that always been a central theme for you?

A very central theme, yes. For a very long time.

We should like now to know something about your personal experiences in the war. You were eighteen when you had to go into the army. Do you remember receiving the message? Was it a shock?

Well... You know the feeling you have if you go into one of those fairground booths where you are pushed in this direction then in that, and you do not know where you are going because you are pushed all the time. You know what I mean? That is the feeling one had when one became a soldier. You were pushed into it, told to do this or that and did it because you had no choice.

Do you remember how it started?

I had to exercise for hours learning the parade step, and how to hold the carbine.

Because my family thought it would be less dangerous, I volunteered to serve in a radio unit, where we had special training in laying telephone lines. I also learned how to climb telegraph poles with climbing irons, and I learned Morse.

The training was in Breslau, where the unit was stationed. I think I owe my health to that training, as I had to become really very strong to endure the long marches with the heavy packs. Sometimes we had a reel of wire on our backs as well.

And then you had to go to the front?

No, I was first sent to the communications zone behind the front in Russia, where I stayed for about six months. Or rather, it must have been occupied Poland. And from there I was moved in a long train journey to the western front.

One incident has stuck in my mind. It was the day before we had to leave. I came back late from a little party with a family I had got to know in the city. There were three beds in our room, and as I had got there first I had the best of them. Now, when I came back late, perhaps having drunk a little wine, I found another soldier in my bed – he had wanted it all along. I was furious and shouted at him, 'Come on, get up. I'm not sleeping in your bed!' Up to then we had got on well, but at that moment I was really angry and started shaking the bed to tip him out. Now he, too, lost his temper, and in this situation – that was very characteristic – he started insulting me, 'Jewboy! Clear off, Jewish pig!' It came out quite suddenly, there had been nothing like it before. Our third room-mate had to separate us.

And the next day was the railway journey.

Yes, I still have an enormously vivid picture in my mind of going to the front... Because we had the heavy rolls of wire, the heavy Morse apparatus and a lot of equipment, we were taken close to the front on a vehicle – a car or a horsedrawn cart, I cannot recollect. Someone was singing. And then far away we saw flashes of light. It was *Trommelfeuer*, a barrage, from a battle to the west. That is the picture I mean: sitting in the car, singing, and seeing the flashes in the distance and hearing the thunder of the guns.

Where was that, roughly?

Vague names sound in my ear. Something like Peron. Yes, Péronne, in northern France. We were a telegraph group, a corporal and eight men, all specialists, who could be attached here or there. And as I drove with my comrades through the night, towards the incessant flashes and the *Trommelfeuer*, someone next to me played the mouth-organ – it probably was a horsedrawn wagon we were riding on. Then we arrived just behind the front, where there were lots of dead horses lying around. And dead people. This whole scene, the bodies, the gunfire, the flashes of light, the sentimental songs, the nostalgic sound of the mouth-organ – that picture is very vivid in my mind.

Do you remember what songs they were singing?

Well, it was always the usual repertoire. The Germans have an enormous number of nostalgic songs which speak of death. I remember one of them [singing]:

> Morgenrot, Morgenrot
> leuchtet mir zum frühen Tod.
> Bald wird die Trompete blasen,
> dann muss ich mein Leben lassen,
> Morgenrot –
>
> [Rosy dawn, rosy dawn,
> luring me to death's dark bourn.
> When the trumpet soon shall blow,

I must leave the life I know.
Rosy dawn –]

and so on.
The Germans have an immense store of that kind of song.
A sort of love song to death.
Yes, it is incredible. I actually once wrote about it, that powerful foreboding of death in German songs – as if they foresaw that they would always lose:

Ich hatt' einen Kameraden,
einen bessern findst du nicht.
Und er starb an meiner Seite...

[A comrade once I had,
a better there never was,
and at my side he died...]

That is very German, immensely German. No other country except Poland has such a sombre sense of itself. The Polish national anthem begins with the incredible words: 'Poland is not yet lost.' Germany and Poland had very similar fates – in the middle, surrounded by stronger neighbours.
You saw dead people for the first time in your life?
Yes, that is right.
Do you remember any other places at the front where you have been? Bapaume, for example, near Péronne?
Yes, it sounds familiar, the same area. But for me they are only grisly memories. Perhaps I was sheltered from the worst because we were a small group, very closely integrated, and I must have been by far the youngest. Cambrai is another of those names; it's on the Somme, isn't it? We probably went from Péronne to the front. It was full of shattered houses.
I don't think I was at the front for longer than a year.
You have described how you arrived there, but do you also remember what it was like to be there?

Yes, a bit. But I must probably have suffered a shock there at some time.

I still remember the dugout. We lived underground, of course. It wasn't just a trench, more like a mole's burrow. I still remember very vividly wooden steps going down, and then there were two rooms deep down under the earth. When there was a near miss lumps of earth came down the steps, the whole thing shook, and anyone outside was hit.

I do not think that I was ever in the most advanced trenches, because our task was to maintain the telegraph lines between the front trenches and headquarters. We were always sent out to mend the wires which were constantly being hit, and sometimes, during a barrage, one simply went into a shell crater and tried to sit it out. Sometimes the wires could hardly be mended, because they were hit again and again. I remember one comrade being wounded next to me, and we had to bring him back. But I never reached the very front line, to my knowledge.

But you did have a sort of shock once.

Yes, on one of those expeditions to repair lines... [A long silence.] I do not know, I have really forgotten.

Was it very dangerous work, mending lines?

One could have been hit, yes. In fact someone was hit.

Do you remember losing any comrades in your group?

No, not losing them. I mean, one saw... For that, I think I should have to go into analysis.

There is another experience I remember very vividly. A school-friend of mine – I still remember his name, Franz Maier – who must have joined up earlier than I did, had been discharged from the army. I was probably still at school. When I went to visit him, he just sat there not saying anything. I did not understand anything, did not understand what could have happened to him. I must have been very innocent, because I had no imagination of what the front was like. I asked him, and he just sat in the garden of his very rich parents, not talking. I could not understand why he did not talk.

It never caught me as badly as that. I probably had a shock, but I... I think that is all I can produce at the moment.

I have a vivid recollection of going to the front, of dead horses and a few dead bodies and that underground shelter... Then there is some feeling of a big shock, but I cannot recollect. I cannot even remember how I got back.

Perhaps I should not say this, but that journey through the night towards the front, moving towards the gunfire and the song, *Morgenrot* or whatever it was, was in a way a very beautiful experience. Then the front itself was a horror. A horror.

Concerning the end of the war, I can only remember being back in Breslau; I have no idea how I got there. First seeing the city and meeting my parents again – all that has gone. But I must have enrolled immediately as a student of medicine, while still in uniform. As a result I was transferred again to a medical corps. The army was not disbanded right away, apparently.

Two organizations remained intact in Germany at that time: the officers' corps and the Social Democratic party, including the trades unions. Perhaps I should add the Catholic church.

Do you remember how the city you left differed from the one you came back to?

Compared to what I know from books, my own memory is completely dead. I only have the image of myself in uniform, being present at operations. I see the surgeon amputating arms and legs, a famous surgeon surrounded by his assistants, of which I was the most junior. That was in Breslau.

The same houses were there, but the world was different?

Yes, the break was enormous. But that is a reconstruction. Now that you are forcing me to think about it, I must say I am surprised myself at how many things about my schooldays, my governesses, are still vivid in my memory, whereas what I have just told you I have had to dig out very slowly. Even my enrolment as a student in 1918 has been buried. So perhaps the war was really a much more shocking experience than I... In any case, I did not even know when I started studying, I had to reconstruct it. But now I am quite certain – Goldstein was the name of the surgeon who carried out the amputations.

I recall that my parents had had an especially elegant uniform made for me, better than the ones handed out by the army. Somewhere there was a photo of my parents with me in uniform – I looked incredibly young, even younger than my age. A child's face looked out of the uniform.

Can you say any more about the difference between Germany in 1914 and 1919? What had changed?

...Your question makes me realize that my own preoccupation with change may have to do with that experience. At the same time, I can now reconstruct the fact that not everything had changed for me personally, because my parents were still there; their fortune, their possessions were still there. Inflation was getting closer, but in 1919 you did not yet feel its full impact; my parents always had enough to eat, and they had their houses. I mean, there was a profound change, but exactly what it consisted of... Well, what is called politics, party strife, played a far bigger role than before.

My difficulty is that I can no longer remember how I reacted, for instance, to the Rathenau murder, the Erzberger murder, the upheavals in political life that were all around me. It is really as if a blind was drawn. I have forgotten my own feeling of that time. It is very strange... my own feeling of that time is a blank.

Even the word 'politics' takes the life out of the experience. It meant such things as that Ebert and Scheidemann became heads of the German Reich. The Social Democrats, who in my parents' circles were probably treated with some contempt as outsiders, were now the most prominent party.

But didn't you have the feeling that, with the Weimar Republic, it was your Germany that had come to power?

Now I have that feeling, of course, but whether I had it then I do not know. I now feel very strongly that the Weimar Republic was really a very good time. Culturally it was a magnificent time.

And the Kaiser was gone.

He had disappeared, yes. For that one was, of course, glad. The whole clique had gone.

Was there any feeling after the war of having been defeated?
That is what a war is about, after all: you win it or lose it –
the outcome is what matters.

What I feel spontaneously is that the feeling of being defeated
was balanced by the good fortune that the Kaiser had gone. That
was a great advance for Germany.

Did you ever have a personal feeling of being defeated, or
was it only that the Kaiser had been defeated?

I cannot say. But a Jewish middle-class person must have felt
differently in that respect from a Gentile middle-class person.
The Gentile German middle classes were enormously embittered,
and that goes for the young people, too. For myself, I am certain
of one thing, and that is that I was not in any way bitter. I was
relieved – but that was the peculiar situation of being a Jew in
Germany.

Because it never was your war.

No, it was never my war. Never. It was always something
I was forced to do and, strangely enough, it seems to me that
that feeling prevailed in the telegraphists' group to which I
belonged. They were all from the working classes, as far as I
remember.

Yes, I cannot express it better than by saying it was a
balance. On balance it was more important that a new Germany
had come than that the old Germany had lost the war.

I studied in Breslau – as I said, both medicine and philosophy.
That must still have been possible. I interrupted my studies in
Breslau twice to go for a semester to Heidelberg and to Freiburg.

I chose medicine mainly because it was the wish of my father,
but I also found it very interesting. My attention had already
been drawn to philosophy at school.

I do not know now how I coped with the double workload.
For I did in fact work myself completely into anatomy, physiology, physics, chemistry, and all those fields because they were
needed for the first medical examination. So I must have worked
very hard. It sounds very odd, but it is possible that my training as a soldier helped. I had been under constant pressure for

days and months, doing long marches with my *Tornister*, my pack, doing drill on the parade ground, cleaning shoes, standing to attention – there was constant pressure to do things. So when I studied medicine I must already have been able to work very hard on my own.

I have very vivid memories of my anatomy and physiology lectures. But at the same time I studied with a much admired and venerated philosophy teacher, Hönigswald.

Philosophy was more your own choice?

Not entirely – I also developed a strong interest in medicine. My doubts only started when I had to go to the clinics. It gradually became more and more difficult to carry on studying both together. For example, one had to go to the ear clinic, and in the women's hospital one had to attend six births – which I did – to get the certificate. I still remember my second birth very clearly: it was a Catholic girl, unmarried, and the child shot out as if from a gun. A very healthy baby; we joked at the time that you needed to be unmarried to have such healthy children.

Where did you live while you studied?

With my parents. In those days that was more usual than today – as it was that all my studies were paid for by my parents.

And why did you go to Heidelberg and Freiburg? Were there especially famous teachers there?

Well, it was still quite normal at that time, and I think it was an excellent institution.

I then had some awful experiences, because I was really not doing enough for medicine any more. Once I was called out in the auditorium of the ear clinic to answer a few questions, and gave some ridiculous answers, because I didn't know the first thing about it. So I gradually decided to give it up; and I also said to myself that I really did not want to become a doctor. I wanted to become a philosopher.

Did the study of medicine have an impact on your thinking?

Yes, a very great impact. You see, sociologists who have not studied medicine speak of society without relating it to the biological aspects of human beings, and I think that is wrong. Sociologists have a defensive attitude towards biology because they fear that otherwise sociology would dissolve into biology. In my view, if you develop a theory about human action, let us say, you also have to know how the organism is built and functions. If you are working out theories of knowledge and know nothing about brain structures, something is wrong. I myself sometimes went into my sociology lectures with a model of the brain to make students understand how human beings are built – because only then can they understand how societies work. I do not thereby reduce sociology to biology.

When did you finish your study of philosophy?

It must have been about 1923–4. I was then in the middle of a difficult period, because at that time my parents' fortune had dwindled through inflation, and I had to maintain them. So after I had my doctorate I went into business. You see, they had houses with fixed rents, so that when the mark was devalued they still had the same nominal income, which meant that they had nothing to eat. I heard by chance of a factory owner who wanted an academic to work with him; he was full of ideas and wanted an academic. That was in Breslau.

What kind of factory was it?

A metal goods factory, with metal furnaces. My special field was pipes. There were pipes of enormously different dimensions, small pipes, big pipes, and I had to learn all the dimensions in which we produced pipes.

That went on for about two years, I'm not quite sure. At any rate, it too was a magnificent experience. My boss sent me round to all the departments. I had to spend one month with the foreman to calculate wages; I had to stand for one month next to the men at the machines; I had to go to the stores to learn all the sizes and kinds of goods we produced. I had to go to the foundry, and in addition I was present every morning when he had all the departments together to give his instructions.

You won't find many other philosophers who have worked in an iron foundry.

Yes, I really do not know how I did all that. For at the same time, after my doctoral viva I was still quarrelling with my supervisor because I had attacked him and he did not want to accept my dissertation. But that is another story.

My main subjects in the examination, to complete the picture, had been philosophy and psychology, and my subsidiary subjects chemistry and art history. After that I went into the factory.

Did not the move to business make you unhappy for a time?

My memory may be selective, but as far as I remember I found the work highly interesting; for a future sociologist those were immensely valuable experiences.

In a practical way, I learned a lot about economics. My view of capitalism was greatly influenced by that factory owner, a very nice person. I first saw a tweed jacket on him, and after that my ambition for years was to get a tweed jacket. He always had a cigarette in the corner of his mouth... He had married the daughter of the former factory owner and was very smart. Once I asked him: 'Tell me, Herr Meerländer', – that was his name – 'why on earth do you do that? You are a rich man and yet you sit here eight hours a day.' Then he took his cigarette from his mouth, smiled and said: 'You know, it's a hunt. A *hunt*. I *must* get this order and the others must not; I must grow, and you shall see: we *shall* grow.' He did grow, but I was no longer there to see it.

Were you useful to him?

Not really, no. I do not think so. I mean, I built up the exports a bit, we got orders for ventilation ducts. That was a speciality of ours; there were export possibilities, with competitors in Sweden who supplied a similar article. So I had to fight for orders against the Swedes. I also hired agents in Romania. It was done by letter. Someone sent a letter asking if he could be an agent for our ventilation ducts, and I asked him to get us a few provisional orders, and so on.

You describe it as if it were fun.

Yes, it was a nice experience. I still remember being invited by the foreman. I never had such a close contact with the working classes as there.

Could you share that hunting fever?

Not really, no. I think my boss's answer was the best I ever had. For it's nonsense that they want to get rich – they *are* rich. It's the thrill of the power struggle, that is the real thing.

Did it not thrill you, too?

No, not at all. I mean, he was a bit of a gambler, that gives the same feeling. But I am not at all a gambler, quite the opposite.

But haven't you a hunting ground, if of a different sort?

The hunt for discoveries, yes – but that is very different. Not a power struggle, because it depends on objective achievement, the demonstrable process.

But there must also be an element of defeating others.

Yes, but with me that came very late, because I did not polemicize. I do it only now. I really wanted to show how it was.

Why did you leave the factory?

Because my parents could live on their own income again. After the inflation and the introduction of the new Reichsmark my father was well off again, and so I decided at once to go back to university.

At that time I also wrote a number of stories based on Greek anecdotes, that I was able to sell. I was very fond of the specific humour of the ancient Greeks, and I always read a lot. I sent some of these anecdotes to the *Berliner Illustrierte*, which accepted them. 'Hurrah,' I thought. 'now I can earn my living as a journalist. I'm going to Heidelberg.' I told my father, 'I'll just go on writing such things and sell them to the *Berliner Illustrierte* – Look, I'm a free man.' He answered, 'If you want to give up a very promising position as a businessman – all right.' He was really very tolerant.

So I went to Heidelberg. Naturally, I never sold another piece to the *Berliner Illustrierte*, but at any rate I was in Heidelberg. I was happy there, gave private lessons in German, I think. Then I must have written to my father to say that my journalistic efforts had not been too successful, and he will have sent me a small monthly allowance.

When was it that you left Breslau?

It must have been 1925–6. I had been to Heidelberg earlier, as a student. But now I had my doctorate, in philosophy and psychology.

I think my experiences in the war, and in commercial life, strengthened my sense of reality. In my thesis of 1923 I tried to make it clear that I no longer believed in a priori thinking. But my research supervisor forced me to insert a proviso that 'validity' was eternal and stood outside the flux of history. I knew even then that that was wrong.

Now I switched to sociology, and in Heidelberg I only came into contact with sociologists, not philosophers. I attached myself to Mannheim, who was not much older than I was. We really liked each other and became good friends. Mannheim was unquestionably brilliant, and at that time at his peak. So he attracted more and more students, away from older professors like Alfred Weber. There was high tension between the two, even though it was expressed in civilized terms.

What was your position at the university, exactly?

A kind of unpaid assistant. I was in the normal intermediate position in a German university career, when you waited to find a professor who would sponsor you to become an unpaid lecturer, called a *Privatdozent*.

Mannheim was one step above. He was already a Privat-dozent and as such had a right to give lectures. But you only got the students' lecture fees. You needed to have money of your own to live like that, and that was the case with Mann-heim: I believe his wife came from a rich Hungarian family.

I myself was something of a middle man between him and the students; I was always better with students than he. I helped him in that way, and he advised me how to pursue my career. He must have given Marianne Weber my name; so one day I received an invitation to her salon. After that, one had free access there.

What sort of a place was Heidelberg at that time?

First of all, a students' town. The students dominated the scene, rather as at Oxford and Cambridge. The townspeople were used to letting rooms to them, and so I lived for years with Fräulein Dürrsamen, who took care of me, in the main street. I can still see the small bedroom and the larger living room before me.

At that time Heidelberg was still under the sway of the students' associations, who wore caps and a ribbon of a particular colour that was the signature of their association. The so-called *Freistudenten*, or free students, who did not belong to a society, were probably a minority, if a militant one. Only free students went to Mannheim – there was a complete separation between left and right.

As a Jew, could you be a member of a students' society with colours?

No. However, there were Jewish associations which tried to imitate them, and I did belong for a time to one of them in Breslau. But they were not taken seriously; they were not entitled to demand satisfaction. I remember from my Breslau time that I was once at a wedding of one of the 'old boys' – I had just been elected one of the first officers and had to put on the whole rigmarole of the cap and so on. A colleague and I found ourselves in this strange uniform in the synagogue, and he whispered to me: 'From one Middle Ages into another.' So you had this very strange situation where Jews who were not admitted or hardly admitted to German students' associations formed their own associations, more or less modelled on the others – and at the same time smiled about it.

There was nothing like that in Heidelberg, of course; there one was just a free student. I spent a great deal of time reading Marx, whom I had never read before. I had heard of Max Weber but did not know anything; so it was all new to me. I was determined to become a *Privatdozent* in sociology, and had to transfer completely to the new field.

What did you know about sociology?

Hardly anything. During my first stay in Heidelberg, Jaspers had told me a bit about what a great figure Max Weber was, so I already had some idea. And after my experiences as a soldier and businessman I probably wanted to get closer to a field of study connected to real life experience.

Heidelberg was a kind of Mecca for sociologists at that time. Although the great Max Weber was dead, his widow was still there, and his brother Alfred, who was a professor of sociology.

Germany already had quite a tradition in sociology; think of Simmel, who only got a professorship shortly before his death, because he was a Jew. There were three or four very famous sociologists like Leopold von Wiese, for example. The flowering of sociology started in the late imperial period, but it had a particular uplift in the Weimar Republic.

How do you explain that?

In the late *Kaiserzeit* it was carried on by liberal bourgeois people like Max Weber, Simmel and others, while in the Weimar Republic – I mean, with the rise of social democracy – people like Mannheim were strongly influenced in their thinking by Marx. That was also true of Max Weber. But Weber had tried to develop a middle-class counter-sociology. Mannheim took up one aspect of Marx's teaching in his sociology of knowledge, and made it into a sociological field. Yes, with the changes in the Weimar Republic a leftist, pinkish sociology grew up.

Were you very ambitious when you went to Heidelberg?

I wanted to have a university career, and in Heidelberg it was quite clear that sociology was the right way for me. I am not sure whether you can call it ambition, but I was quite convinced that this was what I could do well.

Heidelberg was more than ever before a place where one could match one's strength with one's contemporaries and either be reassured or defeated in friendly rivalry with equally intelligent people.

Did you have any higher goal before you? Making Germany a better country, preventing another war, or anything like that?

My strongest feeling then, I think, was of the enormous number of falsehoods that were spread around about human society. I could not agree with all my acquaintances who were in the party because, as I sometimes told them, you were forced to lie.

What I really wanted was to break through the veil of mythologies drawn over our image of society, so that people could act more reasonably and better. For it was clear to me that this partisan thinking prevented people from seeing things. And so Mannheim's central thesis that all thought is ideology was very congenial to me. He put in a more systematic form a feeling I felt all around – the feeling that whatever I read or heard in discussions was full of wishful dreams, wish fulfilments and stigmatizations. And that we need to get a knowledge of our human world which is as realistic as possible.

You had a special aversion for partisan feeling.

I hated the disguise, not the partisanship. I was partisan myself. I hated the feeling that they had to speak in ideologies. On one point I did differ from Mannheim from very early on: whereas he was stuck at the position that everything was ideology, I wanted to go beyond that point to an image of society which is not an ideology; and that I have achieved.

Can you give examples of the kind of mythologies you so disliked?

I came across the first mythology in my childhood, when I saw the Emperor and heard all about the glory of Germany, and read the *Schlesische Zeitung*, the conservative paper in Breslau. I came across the nationalistic propaganda, the war propaganda, which probably played a big part; for when I saw the front there was a very great discrepancy with what some of the war papers said about it. And then in Heidelberg I observed that the partisanship of the left was not much less prone to untrue idealization and ideologies. So my sense of breaking through this veil of concepts goes very far back.

Through my study of biology, chemistry and physics I had a firm idea of science, and what I then came up against in sociology was in sharp contrast to it. On the other hand, I loved sociology, because it promised that kind of breakthrough.

You are right in thinking that this need to strip away the veil was one of my main motives. Many people still resist it now, as they did earlier. I know that I am constantly being mis-understood, because people distort things to fit in with their wishes. I don't go along with that.

Your way of thinking is entirely anti-religious.

Oh yes, of course – or perhaps no, not 'anti'. The answer I usually give is: I am not superstitious. I am in fact very tolerant towards religious people, and not at all 'anti'. But I myself am not superstitious.

Your goals in your thinking were fairly ambitious.

Yes, it is an ambitious goal, and I have only achieved part of it, which makes me a little sad, as I am not sure whether my work will be carried on. I also have a strong feeling that this is not the task of a single person, but the task of many generations. I don't think I can achieve much on my own.

For reasons unknown to me I very early had the feeling of being a part of a chain of generations: I do my bit, take a few steps forward, in a chain of generations. That is what I can do: I have this gift and therefore the duty to make good use of it. I still feel the same today. I see something and have to put it down on paper as well as I can... How it goes on from there is a matter for later generations.

How long did you stay in Heidelberg?

From 1925–6 to 1930.

And your main intellectual reference point there was Mannheim?

That is a bit difficult to say because I was also critical of him. It would be an exaggeration to call him my main reference point. The enormous numbers of discussions going on all over the place were important to me.

When you talk about it like that, it sometimes sounds rather too carefree. You talked with friends, were intellectually stimulated, and disaster was just around the corner.

Well, I do not think I ever thought of disaster as being in the offing. I have just read an interview by Kurt Wolff, where he tells how Mannheim said to him in 1933: 'This whole Hitler thing cannot last more than six weeks. The man is mad.'

That was not my opinion, because I was probably too cautious to make such a firm statement. But I too had no idea that it would last more than ten years. No, no one in Heidelberg realized that disaster was in the offing.

Do you remember when you first heard about the National Socialists?

Certainly, one of Alfred Weber's assistants was a National Socialist, I knew him very well. But he was very civilized, as I was: we were all civilized. Of course, there were street fights, but I can still see Richard Löwenthal, who was then one of the most prominent Communists among the students, in the great hall of Heidelberg University, standing there, a small, very Jewish-looking person, talking to a whole audience of corps students. That, too, was possible. Nothing happened to him. And there was the very civilized Alfred Weber. I do not think he had any idea of what was coming.

Is it not curious that you were not a member of a party while all your friends were? You felt free not to be one – why?

But with my viewpoint, with my need to look through the disguises, how could I have been a member of a party? All their programmes were based on wishful thinking.

But how could you ever influence society without being a member of a party?

I don't think I ever thought about it. I knew that my task was to break through the disguises.

You never wanted to found your own party?

Good gracious, no. It never crossed my mind. Good gracious me. It is an absurd idea, absolutely absurd.

You are reacting almost as if we had insulted you – we apologize. But you did want to influence society.

Yes, certainly. But by establishing a form of knowledge about society which is realistic. That is what I set out to do.

Did you not also want people to share your ideas, to convince them?

You know, in retrospect your question sounds very reasonable, but I do not think I ever thought about how it would be in detail. My task was different.

Was nationalism the main mythology you wanted to unmask?

Nationalism, Communism – whatever you like.

Is every ideology a mythology?

Yes. In my book *What is Sociology?* there is a chapter: 'The sociologist as a destroyer of myths'. That puts it in a nutshell.

Have you never thought that people need myths?

Yes, but then they ought to write poetry, as I have done. I needed myths, too – and paintings.

But many people need myths in daily life: myths about their party, their country, their football club...

People do need myths, but not in order to arrange their social life. It is my conviction that people would live together better without myths. I think myths always come back on one with a vengeance.

So you do not agree with the idea that myths are indispensable in social life?

Why should they be?. Certainly, reality has some extremely unpleasant aspects – for instance, the fact that life is completely meaningless. But one has to face up to that because it is the condition of one's effort to give it a meaning. Only people can do that for each other. Seen in this way, the illusion of a given meaning is harmful.

You do not like illusions.

What do you mean: You do not like illusions? I *know* that they are harmful. Why do you immediately translate that into likes and dislikes? What kind of language is that? I am speaking of knowledge.

If you said one cannot live without fantasies – that's something different.

Is there such a sharp difference between myth and fantasy?

The difference is whether you know that they are fantasies, or whether you regard them as a reality. In the latter case you cheat yourself, and that, of course, one should not do. One should not cheat oneself, and one should not cheat others with one's own myths.

I very sincerely think that we live in a forest of mythologies and that at the moment one of the main tasks is to clear it away. A great springcleaning – that is really what has to be done.

In those years about 1925–6, what were the themes you were most interested in?

Let me think for a moment... I remember that I had a very hard struggle for concentration. And that I gave a talk on the sociology of Gothic architecture, of all things, at Marianne Weber's salon. I concentrated on Gothic architecture because it could be clearly related, in Germany at least, to the development of the towns: each town aimed at having a higher tower than the others, it was a competition between towns. We usually see it as a striving upwards towards heaven, but in reality it was a competition.

At the same time I began my work on the sociology of the change from prescientific to scientific thinking. For this reason I went to Florence, as I saw Florence as the focal point of the whole development. I remember looking for documents on the early Galileo, and on a circle of painters I call the experimental painters, Masaccio, Uccello – perhaps you know of them. They were the turning point, the first painters who worked with perspective. There too I was interested in the general question of how people move from mythological to scientific thinking. In sociology, I still think now, we are stuck in the prescientific phase, and that is why I took an interest in that other turning point: how did they manage in the early fifteenth century to show a three-dimensional space – reality – for the first time on a two-dimensional canvas?

Were these subjects regarded as worthwhile in Heidelberg at that time, or rather eccentric?

As worthwhile. Alfred Weber readily accepted my proposed thesis on the beginnings of the natural sciences.

Did Germany change very much in the five years you were in Heidelberg. Could you compare Germany in 1925 and in 1930?

Well, you noticed, of course, that violence was on the increase, violence in the street battles between National Socialists and Communists. But they were both alien to me – they were just barbarians on the horizon. What one noticed was the increasing hatred.

Did you feel safe in those years?

Perfectly safe – in Heidelberg, that is. Not in Frankfurt, but that was after 1930.

What was Germany like in 1930, politically speaking?

It was a country deeply split, of that one was conscious. On one hand there was a very powerful working-class movement, above all the Social Democrats and the trade unions, with a circle of intellectuals at the universities and elsewhere, and on the other hand the massive block of the middle classes, the middle and upper classes, who were opposed to the Social Democratic party with a bitterness that is hardly imaginable today. And you knew that it would be difficult for someone who had leftist views to get an unbiased hearing in court, in Länder such as Bavaria, if a political matter was involved.

The right were only too conscious of their power, and one could see the balance of power gradually inclining in their favour. While immediately after the First World War the Social Democrat party and perhaps also the liberals had been very powerful, during the Weimar Republic as a whole there was a gradual swing to the right – whether it was the relatively moderate right represented by Stresemann's Deutsche Volkspartei, or more conservative; or it might be the extreme right, or the Catholic Centre party, which was also moving to the right.

There was a real bisection of the country. That did not mean that people with different positions on the party spectrum at the university did not speak to each other. But you could feel the power of the right gradually increasing. All the same, no one in my circle imagined anything remotely like what later happened.

This whole mood went together with a kind of elation over the cultural achievements that were then possible. When Mannheim and I came to Frankfurt, we found ourselves at the centre of an extremely lively and highly productive intellectual circle; that is to say, culturally it was an eminently fruitful time. Among the big names in Frankfurt were Goldstein, the psychiatrist, Wertheimer, the main founder of Gestalt psychology, Löwe, the economist – it was an extremely stimulating climate. We did not imagine that there would be more than a slow shift in the balance of parliamentary power towards the right, and did not feel an immediate threat to our whole lives. We worked, each in his own field, with the prospect of a very fruitful future.

Was there no sign at all of a threat?

Only in 1932 did I begin to feel there could be a real threat, because the whole country was full of private armies. That is something which you cannot imagine: the Communists had a private army, the Social Democrats had a private army, the Nazis had their SA and the conservative bourgeoisie their 'Stahlhelm'. I remember very distinctly that in 1932 I became aware of the increasing threat of violence in the form of what were called *Saalschlachten* – assembly-hall battles. If a Communist speaker, shall we say, wanted to speak in a beer-cellar, the Nazis turned up and broke up the meeting, and vice versa. The more moderate private armies did not go so far, but you could see them walking through the streets – the Stahlhelm, for example: rather stout men in uniform.

In considering the history of the Weimar Republic, I do not think enough attention has been given to the breakdown of the state's monopoly of violence. And one can see very clearly why it was breaking down: because the Reichswehr, that is, the army, was itself firmly in the hands of the right. It was not a neutral instrument of the state, but an instrument of the right.

What was your own position in the political spectrum?

Well, I was not a man of the right. All my friends were of the left, and in this confrontation I sympathized with the left.

Which party did you vote for?

I did not vote.

Why not?

Because... for me the language of politicians was so transparently full of assertions I could see to be wrong... I sympathized thoroughly, of course, with what the left did in the struggle and I did my best to help. But the left's ideology was unrealistic. The Social Democrats and the unions believed – like my father – in the constitutional state. That is, they were convinced that right would always decide the issue and that violence had no place in the state. That is why the Social

Democrat party was against the Communists: they did not want
a revolution; they did not want to use force.

I still remember very vividly how I went to a trade union one
day to speak about my understanding of the situation. I pointed
out that the private armies were gradually becoming more important than parliamentary elections. I closed my little talk somewhat dramatically with the question: 'Gentlemen, what measures
have you taken to defend this fine union building if you are
attacked?' The answer was a deep silence. I knew why, of course,
and then they admitted it: they had never thought of such an
eventuality. Perhaps that gives you an idea of the whole situation.

Did you yourself believe in the constitutional state?

No, my sense of reality stopped me doing so. I had already
come to realize something that was later to play a much bigger
part in my thinking: that law cannot function without the
backing of physical force.

So you believed rather in power?

I did not *believe* in power, but I gave a sociological, realistic
appreciation of the situation. Forgive me, but I cannot permit
such a way of expressing it. I did not *believe* in power.

*Perhaps 'believe' is not the right word, but at any rate it was
your opinion that power was decisive.*

Physical power, one should say. I saw clearly that law without
the backing of one kind of physical violence or another cannot
function, that the state cannot function once its control of
physical force is destroyed. And I saw – perhaps more clearly
than present-day historians see it – that the whole balance of
power in Germany was changing, because the army was in the
hands of the traditional conservatives and was not the instrument of the government.

Did you talk much about these things with others?

No, but I took them seriously enough to have the discussion
with the union. And they told me, 'We are at a disadvantage
because there aren't enough professional officers in our private
army, the "Reichsbanner Schwarz-Rot-Gold" – all the professional officers are in the other camp – and it's because we
haven't got enough money.' Then they came out with the

question of whether I could get money for them from rich Jews, to bring their troops up to the mark. I answered, 'Sorry, but I haven't any good connections among rich Jews.'

We do find it strange that you did not become more politically involved. Was that not very difficult at such a dangerous time?

Well... I did not have the illusion that I could make much difference.

But did you not write newspaper articles, or anything like that?

I am not a politician. And do you not understand that I recognized so much of that as illusion? I did not share those illusions.

Those are rational, intellectual considerations. Emotionally, is it not rather different?

My emotions were directed at not letting me fall for the current illusions. There I was very committed. I avoid the word 'rational'; but I can distinguish between a realistic action and a less realistic one. That's how I would see it.

Were you a pessimist?

No. Pessimism and optimism are, again, categories which do not fit. I cannot work with them. They are, if I may say so, too crude. I was neither pessimistic nor optimistic; I tried to the best of my ability to be realistic.

Did you feel an allegiance to democracy, the parliamentary system?

I would not have talked of 'democracy', but of course I was profoundly against a dictatorship.

It is still difficult to understand why you kept yourself so aloof.

I did not hold myself aloof! I did what was possible. Please don't take it amiss if I ask you: what would you have done?

Voted, at least.

And then you would have had the illusion that you had done something?

At least the minimum in a democracy.

Well, in that situation it was obvious that voting was not the most important thing. It would have given emotional relief, nothing more.

Perhaps it is different in the Netherlands today; but at that time it was very realistic to draw attention to the importance of reflecting on strategies of violence. That was certainly not holding oneself aloof.

Have you ever voted in your life?

Possibly, I cannot recollect at this moment. What is certain is that I never voted in England, where I was only made a British subject late in my life. Whether it was always like that in Germany I no longer know. But I followed political events with great interest. When Hitler made a speech in Frankfurt, I went along.

That must have been at the end of 1932 or early 1933. A big speech by Hitler was announced, and I was burning with curiosity to see him in the flesh. But that was dangerous, because I was recognizable as a Jew. On the other hand, with a suitable disguise my features could pass as aristocratic. If I took off my spectacles, wedged a monocle in my eye, put on a little hunter's hat and different clothes, I was a different person. And so, accompanied by two towering, very Aryan-looking students, I walked between the rows of SS.

It was fascinating... The Führer kept an excited crowd waiting for two hours; they sang patriotic songs, and sometimes I had to move my mouth, because I could not be the only one sitting there in silence. Once I left the assembly for a moment and found myself suddenly face to face with another participant who was a National Socialist. He started back – so did I; and then I glanced over my shoulder, as he did, and walked away. A very curious moment – but then the Fuhrer arrived. He was really an uncommonly good speaker. One thing above all else has stayed in my mind: how he blessed the children at the end. I'd never seen that before! He had the children come up to him, laid his hand on their heads and talked to them. And the crowd roared with enthusiasm.

I went to such meetings to orientate myself, to gain understanding and to see with my own eyes.

Did Hitler say anything about the Jews in that speech?

He made a few anti-Semitic remarks, about the 'dirty Jews', but he did not say he wanted to have them all killed. Perhaps I had, more than you, the feeling that as an individual one could do very little. Even then I had a certain idea of chains of interdependence: how the individual is bound by reciprocal dependence on others.

Can you recall what Hitler spoke about?

No, not in detail. I know that he talked about the glorious future: how great Germany would be and how pernicious the present regime was.

When you heard him, did it arouse strong feelings in you?

I thought him dangerous. Very dangerous.

Were you afraid?

I don't think so.

Because he was not yet in power.

I was not really afraid even when they came to power. If I had been afraid, I should not have gone to the meeting. Imagine: someone would only have needed to shout 'Jew' and I should have been beaten up. I had an intense need to know what was going on, and that does not go with being afraid.

Why did you want to know what was going on?

Because I think it is one of the most important tasks of human beings: if they want to arrange their lives better than they are now, they have to know how things are connected together. I mean that quite practically, since otherwise we act wrongly. The whole misfortune of people now is that they often let themselves be guided by unrealistic ideas.

Such as?

There was once great enthusiasm for Communism. People sacrificed their lives for it – and look what has come of it. There was enthusiasm for liberalism, American presidents and economists still believe in it – and are they any more able to cure our economic ills? They act as if they knew the answers, on the basis of ideals, but in reality they do not know how the economy or states function.

There should be more people like myself who are not afraid of what they discover. People are obviously afraid that they will find out something unpleasant if they think realistically about themselves. Take Freud: he wanted to find out in his own way how things really are, regardless of what people had said before him. And that is the task of a scientist, in the social sciences as in the natural sciences. That is the ethos of a scientist.

Back to politics. Had many of your university colleagues disappeared by 1933?

Yes; students, too. Most of our students were leftist or very leftist. It must have been in February 1933 that I suddenly realized that I ought to look in our department to see if any compromising papers had been left behind. So I went back and found the membership list of the 'Red Students' Group'; masses of damaging things were lying about, such as a complete list of the names of our students. I looked through all the rooms in the department and took away everything that looked in any way suspicious. When the SS came for me some days later so that I would hand over the department to them, I was very impertinent, as I knew they would not find anything. They came to my rooms to fetch me, and then I, Norbert Elias, was driven through Frankfurt in an open jeep, a Nazi flag beside me. I was responsible for the department, and so I had the key. I can still see the scene before me. An SS lieutenant looked at the shelves of books and pulled out Marx: 'Aha, Marx – of course! These filthy Communists.' When I asked him, 'What are you actually looking for?', he replied, 'That's none of your business.'

It was the so-called 'Marxburg' – the building of the famous Institut für Sozialforschung, where the sociology department of Frankfurt University had rented the ground floor. After I had handed over the keys they strictly forbade me to enter the building ever again; then I was allowed to go home.

Did you go back there?

A week later I talked to the porter at the back entrance, and he told me the Nazis were digging: the building, belonging to the group around Horkheimer, stood opposite the Social Democrat *Volksstimme*, and they had the idea – just as in a detective story – that there must be an underground passage between the *Volksstimme* and Horkheimer's institute. Which was completely absurd, as Horkheimer was not a Social Democrat. But their imaginations ran along those lines.

By then I was no longer an assistant, although my salary was paid until October 1933. But that was probably arranged by the university.

When did you decide to leave Germany?

It must have been in March or April 1933. I laid plans with a student and good friend of mine that she would drive me to Switzerland, so that I could look around for a university post. She was Grete Freudenthal, who had a car, and she did take me to Basle, Zurich and Berne, where I asked the few people I knew about a possible post. In vain.

I no longer know exactly when I left Germany. I think I first visited my parents, then I went to Paris.

What did your parents say about your decision?

Well, they wished me success... So off I went to Paris. And in 1935 I left Paris because I had no prospect of getting a post at a French university.

Were those two years an important part of your life?

That is difficult to say. They were a very stimulating part of my life. I mean, one was thrown back completely on one's own resources; one sat about in cafés and had no plan for one's life.

Did you have any money?

My father must have given me some. And then I opened a small factory, for toys, bought some machines and lost all the money I had. I did the rounds of the Paris stores and tried to sell them our things. There was an elephant on wheels, a jumping jack – I have forgotten the details.

Did you design the models yourself?

Oh no. I had two partners, working-class people, Communists from Germany, who had also left. One of them was a well-known writer, Ludwig Turek, and the other an acquaintance of mine from Frankfurt, a sculptor who could draw and do the designs. There were all kinds of nice incidents; for instance, I remember Turek being presented to André Gide. This meeting between a genuine German proletarian and the very cultivated Gide must have been highly fascinating. Turek told me about it later.

The three of us were able to live from this enterprise for about nine months. My job was selling, and deciding which models would sell best, as I knew the buyers from my trips around the stores.

In the same period I wrote two essays – not my very first, but almost the first that were printed: the piece on the Kitsch style and another on 'The expulsion of the Huguenots from France'. And they were published, one of them in Holland. The Querido Verlag had a kind of émigrés' journal, edited by Klaus Mann, and I had met Mann by chance in Paris. On that occasion he asked me to write something for him.

I also received a grant from a Dutch foundation, the Steun-fonds, through Professor Frijda, and had links to the École Normale Supérieure; but they had no money.

Did you miss Germany?

Well, I had always had a deep love of France. I loved French culture and spoke almost perfect, accent-free French at that time – unlike England, where I never lost my accent. I loved France and loved Paris, but that made it all the more dispiriting that not a single French person invited me to their house. They simply do not do it. Or rather, only one of them did: Alexandre Koyré, an excellent historian of ideas, of Russian-Jewish origins. I had some contact with him.

In which quarter of Paris did you live?

Probably Montparnasse; I lived in a hotel. It was very nice to go dancing at the Apache, near the Bastille, and to sit at the cafés of Montparnasse. You could eat very well at cheap restaurants, and meet everybody – except French people. But at the same time it was a very difficult time, the only time I ever went hungry because my money had run out.

All the same, we did not lose heart. One simply lived from day to day and hoped for the best, as long as the money lasted.

I remember the two or three days when I simply could not get hold of any money; I asked someone I knew, who was sitting next to me in a café, to buy me a coffee and rolls.

Why did you leave France?

Because the situation was hopeless there. No future. Two friends of mine from Breslau who were now living in England said to me, 'Why don't you come to England?' And I replied, 'I can't. I don't know any English,' – that is to say, at best, I could read a little. But then I went all the same. I visited my parents, and I still vividly remember my father buying me a portable typewriter as a leaving present. I still have it; I took it to England. That was in 1935 – the last time I was in Germany before the war.

And probably the last time you saw your parents.

No. They visited me in London, in 1938. You will not believe it, but they came in 1938. That was still possible.

Did you find Germany very much changed on your last visit? By then there were far more National Socialists.

Certainly, and yet... it is a big country. One saw more swastikas in the street, perhaps, but all the other people who were not National Socialists were still there.

But were you not treated unpleasantly at the German border, for example?

Germany is a very orderly country. Things were very well ordered at that time. At the time of the street battles there had been naked force; but after they came to power, Germany became orderly again, a constitutional state.

National Socialist Germany?

I did not express myself clearly. Conditions in Germany were still well ordered, and the feeling that it was a constitutional state where no harm could come to you was deeply rooted. Think of it – even my parents were not afraid enough to leave Germany.

Did it not feel like a dangerous country?

It was all dreadful; it was, of course, terrible. A dictator, Hitler... one felt real contempt for him, and it was bad that this man was ruling Germany. But that did not mean that people like my parents – or like myself, when I travelled through Germany – were in acute fear for their lives. Such an idea is always a projection from later; you see, the National Socialists themselves only slowly got to the idea of the 'Final Solution'. They had not planned the gas chambers from the first, it was a gradual process. So how could we have had an inkling of it?

It seems so incredible that your parents visited you in London. They were safe there – and yet they went back.

But they said, 'Why should we go away? All our friends are in Breslau, and in London we don't know anyone.' I can still hear my father's words as if he were saying it now: 'Ich habe nie etwas Unrechtes getan, was können sie mir tun?' ('I have never done anything wrong. What can they do to me?').

I begged them to stay. I did not want them to go back to Breslau, as I had the feeling they were in danger there. I begged them with all my power. But they did not understand me, they were old and had their familiar life in Breslau; you cannot uproot such people. I still blame myself today that I did not have the power to convince them. My father also asked: 'What should I live on here?' And I could only answer that I would help them, that I would try to earn more.

You could not force him.

No, I could not force him. That was the last time I saw my parents.

I still remember very clearly... Of course, I shall never get over it. I'll never get over it...

So you realized how urgent it was that they should stay.

Yes. It was 1938, and in 1938 one knew, naturally... The 'Crystal Night' had already happened – all kinds of bad things. But no one yet knew anything about the concentration camps.

But Dachau already existed?

Jews were not yet being systematically deported.

Dachau was for political prisoners.

And apart from that, I was deeply involved in writing my book on the civilizing process.

And you never saw your parents again.

My mother wrote to me in 1940 to tell me that my father had died. She wrote me letters, I still have them. Then she disappeared, to Auschwitz... Excuse me for a moment.

When and where did you decide to write the book on the civilizing process? In Germany? In Paris?

To be able to answer that I shall have to say something about the strange dilemma one is in if one is thrown completely off one's path in life. On one hand I knew that I had to work on it, to open up a career for myself again; I was still young enough for that. On the other hand, even in Paris, it had been very pleasant to have to live from day to day. It may go against your ego ideal, but such a life has its pleasing side – as if a burden has been taken away.

When I arrived in London, I naturally had no income. But there was a Jewish refugees' committee that was willing to support me. I told them that I could only get back to my career if they paid me enough money to write a book: they replied that that was quite unrealistic, because my English was still very weak, and I should have to write the book in German. Finally, they allocated me a small amount, just enough not to go hungry and to be able to afford a room. That was about all.

You lived in London?

Yes. I discovered the library of the British Museum, now the British Library, and from then on my life consisted of my getting up in the morning and spending the whole day at the British Museum, with a snack at a nearby café. Of course, I also had some friends. It was a life I very much enjoyed. I knew that for the present I had no future, but I could browse in the British Museum – or more exactly, in the library catalogue: and whenever I saw a title that interested me I asked for the book and read it. My ideas of what I would write about were rather vague at first, but through browsing I gradually got on to a trail that seemed very promising.

Which way did your ideas lead you?

They were very unclear, but I had acquired a lot of know-ledge, which generated a wealth of associations as I read. That

Norbert Elias in his middle years

is how I came across the books on etiquette. I once ordered one of them by chance; I think it was Courtin, and I found it thoroughly exciting. It was exciting because I knew that contemporary psychologists took the view that one could only arrive at a convincing picture of human attitudes by measuring the attitudes of present-day people, while nothing, and certainly nothing reliable, could be inferred from the standards of behaviour of people in the past. Now I suddenly had material that showed how different standards were in earlier times and allowed reliable statements to be made on how they had changed.

So I began my book *The Civilizing Process* with a clear awareness that it would be an implicit attack on the wave of studies of attitudes and behaviour by contemporary psychologists. For academic psychologists – not the Freudians – believed strictly that one had to have someone in front of one here and now, one had to measure the person's attitude by questionnaires and other quantitative methods, to be able to say anything certain about it. And by this method it is, of course, quite impossible to get a view of the present standard as something that has developed. They always proceeded as if the results of tests with present-day people would enable them to draw direct conclusions about people in general.

I was quite sure that that was wrong, that it was simply an attempt to apply physical or biological ways of proceeding to human beings. The whole process of the transformation of people is hidden from view. That, I would say, was my key experience.

Which keywords did you use when ordering books?

When I came across an interesting title... In Frankfurt I had already worked on the eighteenth century in France and written the first draft of *The Court Society*. So I was interested in manners from the start.

In the British Museum I felt completely at home; after six months I knew at least 20 per cent of the regular users. I remember an old, somewhat fat Catholic priest, who visited the library just as regularly as I did, and was working on a Catholic dictionary – from A to Z, day by day. I think he had just reached L.

When I arrived at the library, ten minutes later the library employee would bring the pile of books I had ordered to my table, and then began the joy of browsing; and if I found a possibly interesting reference in a footnote, I went straight to the catalogue and ordered it.

Although there were about 150 people sitting in the reading room, there was a hushed atmosphere; it was pleasant and relaxing to work there for year after year. I went on doing so after my book was finished. In fact, I went to the British Museum until I left England. I worked for exactly three years on *The Civilizing Process*.

Did you do something else as well, or concentrate entirely on the book.

I did nothing else.

Was it a good time?

Well, of course I had all kinds of worries. For instance, that was the time when the situation in Germany was getting worse and I was very afraid for my parents. I was also in the dark about my own future. I had found a publisher in Breslau, but

while I was still writing the book he had to leave the country
because he was a Jew. So I was forced to look for a new
publisher, and my father had to redeem the proofs of the first
volume from the printer. So there were a lot of growing worries
– but in the British Museum I could concentrate completely on
my work. Despite all the worries.

And your grant went on being paid, without a time limit?

Yes, I had no fixed deadline. Every six months I had a talk
with a man from the refugees' committee, who asked how I
was getting on and when the book would be ready. And when
I had finished the first volume, I had to tell him that I was
now writing the second. 'Fine,' he answered, 'fine. If you think
two volumes are needed, we'll do two volumes.'

*In your work, were you influenced by your experience of
the English way of life?*

Probably, but I was hardly aware of it. Certainly, the differences between the English and German standards of behaviour
must have struck me very early on... So I wrote the book completely unaware that it lay quite outside the range of interest
of other people. To me the subject seemed of utmost interest.

*Why did you take France as your model to demonstrate
something about societies in general? After all, you knew German
society much better.*

At that time I really did know a great deal about French
society. And the first part of *The Civilizing Process* is about
Germany as well, the development of the antithesis between
'culture' and 'civilization', that I then compared to the French
concept of civilization. I had done very little work on England.

*France and Germany are old enemies. Did your choice have
something to do with that?*

Your guess is as good as mine... only my analyst would
know. I have no idea. The only thing I can say is, although I
identified strongly with the German tradition, I had from early
on a deep love of French culture.

That I myself fought against the French in the war did not
affect my consciousness very much. It is strange: I was never
interested in them as the enemy, never had that feeling.

Did you want to use the example of France to clarify something about German society?

Yes. I thought, and still do, that with the first part of my *Process* book, where I discuss the German preference for 'culture' and the French for 'civilization', I made an important contribution to clarifying a problem which is very much in vogue at present – the problem of national mentalities. I already did that then. I did not merely note that the national identity of Germans is different from the French, but explained *why* it is different.

That was my first step towards what I believe to be one of my most important insights: that the structure of societies, as of mentalities, can only be ascertained by systematic comparisons.

What was it you wanted to make clear about the German national mentality?

One of the decisive features of the German development is that the barrier between the nobility and the bourgeoisie was much higher, even at court, than in France. In Germany the court aristocracy spoke French, and the middle classes had their own elite, which absorbed very little of the civilized manners of the nobility. The effects of that are still felt today. I was recently in a radio studio, and there you can say in a broadcast such things as, 'That would leave you sitting on your bare arse.' I don't think such a thing would be possible in France or England. In German you can be much coarser than in English or French, and the reason is that the German middle classes never, or only in a very peculiar way, took over models of behaviour from the court.

Even today, French culture and civilization have kept something of the elegance of the court; in the cadences of French speech you can still hear an echo of a court society. Take, for instance, the formula at the end of a letter... 'je vous prie de croire, cher Monsieur...' etc., whereas in German you have the pedantic, bureaucratic 'mit vorzüglicher Hochachtung', and even that is being dropped now.

In your account, did you also want to say something about Germany in the 'thirties?

Yes... a bit. I always had the impression that the extreme lack of inhibition of which Germans are capable is bound up in part with the fact that German culture in the middle and lower classes was only slightly influenced by a stage in the civilizing process that was very important in England and France – the aristocratic stage. I still do not know to what extent the urban patriciate exerted a civilizing influence in Holland.

But Germany did have an aristocracy.

Certainly, but it was dispersed over many small courts and a few big ones, without a central court. The whole relation to the bourgeoisie was different. To give one example: in *Werther*, Goethe describes how Werther accidentally blundered into a social gathering of his patron, a count, and how the count took him aside and gave him very politely to understand that offence was being taken at the presence of a commoner; Werther had to leave. So whereas in France and England a fusion of bourgeois morality and aristocratic good manners occurred, in Germany the barrier between the two was much higher; the German national character was shaped far more by the middle classes.

The German super-ego and ego ideal always left the middle classes, the lower classes and the peasants more room for outbreaks of violence than the English or French patterns, for example.

It seems to us that, fundamentally, you were trying to explain the violence of Germany – the fact that it was a dangerous country.

No, I should never have said that. But there was a dangerous potential, of course. There was certainly such a potential.

So the book The Civilizing Process *also fits into the time when it was written. It is not only a book about France in the eighteenth century, but a book written in London by a German refugee on the eve of the Second World War.*

Undoubtedly there is a connection between the two. At that time the whole problem of civilization had become very acute. But at the same time I had the feeling that I would have been false to my task as a scholar had I not described it in a distanced way. I wanted to develop a theory whose scope went beyond an explanation of present events. It was certainly not my task to accuse – I wanted to show that as a sociologist one could give valid and durable explanations.

How would you apply your own theory to events in Germany between, say, 1930 and 1940? In the Weimar Republic private armies come to the fore and the state monopoly of violence grows weaker and weaker, and people behave in a more and more uncivilized way to each other. Then the National Socialists come to power, the state grows ever stronger and more unified, and law and order prevail in Germany once more. At the same time, people behave more barbarically than ever before. In other words: what kind of relation is there between the civilizing process and the totalitarian state?

As far as Germany is concerned... unlike the French, Dutch or English, the Germans lived under an absolutist regime from the sixteenth/seventeenth centuries to the First World War. Even under the Kaiser the princes were very prominent; although there were already parliaments, they appointed the ministers.

Then the old ruling class was swept away by the defeat of 1918, and after the so-called revolution you suddenly found a personality structure attuned to obedience and self-constraint in relation to a strong ruler, existing in a state where – if I may exaggerate a little – the outward part of the super-ego had fallen away. That is why many Germans in the Weimar Republic began to call for a strong man – the strong man who would restore to them the possibility of controlling themselves. They had never thought of doing that on their own. I exaggerate again; but the same thing can be observed today in the Russians – they had a Tsar and were used to feeling the whip, and now they have a red Tsar who goes on using external compulsion if they do not obey.

Such a regime does not lead to the formation of a super-ego – or, to put it more exactly, it does not lead to the formation of a super-ego in certain spheres. One therefore needs to supplement the Freudian concept of the super-ego by adding that the super-ego can be uneven or it can have gaps. For instance, it can be very strong with regard to the family, sexuality and so on, and be absent in the political area. That was really the case in Germany.

And, of course, there was also the class struggle; on this point the Marxian model is entirely apt. The end of the war in 1918 brought an increase in the power of the working classes which was intolerable to the mass of the German petty bourgeoisie and the nobility; it took away their whole feeling of self-worth. That came on top of the special structure of a conscience that was very strong as regards some aspects of morality, but hardly developed with regard to politics. So the parliament was called a 'talking shop', for instance, and 'compromise' was a term of abuse in German.

And in the end they got their strong man.

Exactly.

Do you believe that an absolutist ruler is good for a civilizing process?

An absolutist ruler can be good for the civilizing of an elite; it depends on the stage of development of the society. In the seventeenth century the absolutist ruler had a great influence on the development of self-constraint among courtiers, in that he forced the nobility to transform themselves from warriors into courtiers; and court life demanded a high degree of self-restraint.

In Germany, by contrast, people never got the chance to deal with conflicts without violence: all conflicts were settled by commands from above. But parliamentarianism is essentially a means of regulating conflicts without recourse to violence, and that the Germans had never learned. It requires enormous self control. The techniques needed for this cannot be developed under an absolutist regime.

If the two regimes are compared, was not imperial Germany really more civilized than Hitler's Reich?

Yet, considered relatively it undoubtedly was. Compared to Wilhelmine Germany the Third Reich was a vulgarization.

Then it might perhaps have been better for Germany if the Kaiser had stayed in power.

I think so, too. In that case Hitler would probably never have come – although one cannot be sure: in Italy the King called in Mussolini. And apart from that, the German crown prince was unfortunately a particularly stupid person.

On the other hand, it is very characteristic of the dependence of the German conscience on external compulsion that Ebert, the Social Democrat, was prepared to accept a son of the crown prince or another of the Kaiser's sons on the throne, if the Kaiser and the very unpopular crown prince abdicated. Foolishly, the imperial house rejected this suggestion. So if Ebert had had his way Germany would have retained a Kaiser. And at that time he was the leader of the strongest political party!

Different stones in the mosaic are falling into place: it was in the Hitler period that you wrote about Louis XIV, and that was in some way connected to the Kaiser.

All these experiences played a part. But you should not overlook the fact, of course, that I was also aiming to elaborate a scientific theory about things that had been lying fallow up to then.

And the book The Civilizing Process *came out in 1939.*

Yes, I was unbelievably lucky. First the publisher disappeared without paying the printer – my father had to bear the cost. Then my father, like all Jews, was gradually stripped of his control over his wealth; he had to get permission from the authorities to pay for the printing of the second volume from his account. And when the second volume was ready, I managed to find a publisher in Switzerland who was prepared to publish the book if he was sent the proofs. So my poor father had to go back to the Nazi authorities and ask for an export licence for the printer. He achieved all that. Without my father's help I should not have been able to publish the book. I often think that it was only saved by a hair's breadth.

The first volume came out in 1938, I think, and the second in 1939. I no longer know how many copies were printed. But when I visited the publisher after the war, he said to me: 'Look, it's filling up my cellar. Couldn't we pulp it? No one wants to buy it.'

Do you recollect the start of the Second World War?

I remember Chamberlain returning from Munich – 'peace, peace' – that I remember. And the glorious spring of 1940, when the assault in the west began. By then I had a post at the London School of Economics, with which I was evacuated to Cambridge. There we led the most peaceful of lives, punting on the river, and drinking coffee and tea in a nearby village. It was a thoroughly peaceful 'phoney war'.

I stayed in Cambridge for some months, until I was interned with the other Germans and taken to the Isle of Man. My internment, which lasted eight months, was in some ways very fruitful for me, because I could practise giving lectures in English. There were other people from the LSE in the camp. C. P. Snow, the writer, and the sociologist Ginsberg helped me to get out.

After my return to Cambridge I got more and more access to English people and English society. I made friends with C. P. Snow, who gave a weekly reception in Christ's College. The Glucksmans, friends from earlier days, were in Cambridge too. That was the phase when I received my first, vivid impressions of English culture and civilization.

How long did you stay in England?

Up till about 1970, I should think. It was a very gradual, sliding disengagement.

In practice I lived there from 1935 until 1975, forty years, only interrupted by my stay in Ghana. So it's no wonder that the English tradition and civilization have left deep traces in my thought.

Did you ever feel yourself to be English?

No – quite impossible. I felt like a British citizen, but that is different. No English person would say I am English. An Englishman is somebody born in England.

Have you a British passport?

I have British nationality. But I could never describe myself as an Englishman.

Have you still got German nationality?

No, although I could get it any time I wanted.

There were many German intellectual emigrants in England at the same time as you, Mannheim, for example. Were you in contact with them?

I was still on a good footing with Mannheim, but our contact was no longer close. When I saw him for the last time he had just been give a chair specially created for him, as Professor of the Sociology of Education. That was a foundation stone for this whole field in England.

A very good friend of mine was the psychoanalyst Fuchs, who had called himself Foulkes, and whom I had known in Frankfurt. For two or three years we had a small working group at his house, preparing, if you like, for the group analysis movement he wanted to set up. I was the only sociologist in the group; all the others were psychiatrists. But that was probably after the war.

Did Maxwell Jones of the Therapeutic Society have anything to do with it?

I knew him, but he was part of a different tendency. He was experimenting with a self-regulating group of, I think, minor offenders. Once or twice I visited his hostel, to observe a psychodrama; it was very impressive.

Then there was the group at the Tavistock Clinic, Bion and so on. The Tavistock people had a much more Kleinian orientation, if that means anything to you. Melanie Klein was, in fact, the mother of English psychoanalysis, as so many English analysts were analysed by her. Fuchs was closer to Anna Freud than to Melanie Klein – there was a strong rivalry, if not exactly animosity, between the two women.

Fuchs succeeded in founding a school of group analysis, that is, he transferred individual psychoanalysis to groups. In such an enterprise close collaboration with sociologists was of utmost importance, and I was the sociologist. In the first edition of his book on group analysis, Fuchs expresses his thanks to me. I think I had a significant influence on the theory of this kind of group therapy. I am even now a founder member of the Group Analytic Society, and receive all their material without paying a subscription.

What did your influence on Foulkes consist of, exactly?

A central point of my thinking, that I passed on to him and that he applied to the technique of group analysis, was the realization that individual and society cannot be separated, that they merely represent two different levels of observation. Group processes have certain peculiarities that are distinct from individual processes, but one must always consider both levels.

By then I had written a second little book, *The Society of Individuals*, in which I tried to make it clear that while a society consists of individuals, the social level has its own regularities, that cannot be simply reduced to individuals. This idea I then applied to group analysis.

Somewhat later I myself conducted a number of groups. I underwent a training in group analysis and for about a year attended a training group under Fuchs.

Did you also undergo individual analysis?

Yes, that was in the same period, after the war. It was very difficult for me, as I did not have enough money. Nevertheless, I was taken on by a very good, orthodox Freudian woman analyst – more in the direction of Anna Freud. I really did part of my growing up in the orthodox tradition.

Can you tell us why you went into analysis?

Well... the most immediate reason was that I wrote very slowly. I was unhappy that I did not produce more, although I had so many ideas.

The analysis went on for several years, I've forgotten exactly how long. There were a number of breaks, when I could not pay for the sessions. The longest gap was about half a year, and soon after that my analyst died. That certainly did not help.

Was your difficulty in writing helped by the analysis?

I'm not aware that my life was changed by it. But perhaps that is a successful analysis – when you go away with the feeling that it has not helped at all, that you have done it all yourself.

I do not know what effects it had on me. I can only say one thing, that the death of my analyst was very traumatic for me – a repeat of the traumatic death of my mother. But since

Adult education in London, shortly after the
Second World War (Elias far right)

then I have managed on my own. That is another conviction of mine – that analysis is a great help and sometimes quite indispensable, but that one should manage on one's own as far as possible.

When did you leave London?

It was in 1954. I had been working for some years in adult education. Now I received two offers of lectureships in sociology, one from Leicester and another from Leeds. Characteristically, both came from people who were themselves refugees, but younger than I was, so that they had been educated at English universities. I decided in favour of Leicester, where Neustadt, who came from Odessa, had a chair. It was one of the new sociology departments that were being set up in England at that time. I helped to build up the department in Leicester.

Were you sorry to have to leave London?

Yes, certainly; but Leicester was a pretty, clean, medium-sized city, and had the additional advantage that one could travel to London and back in a day.

And there you built up a department.

To a considerable extent, yes. I had good contact with the students and very much liked teaching the introduction to sociology. That is one of the great disappointments of my life, that I developed an excellent introductory course for the first year of study, that I taught for about ten years; and then, when I left, it was watered down more and more and went into decline.

I also took care to ensure that only really gifted people became lecturers, which had the very curious result that, after London, Leicester was the main supplier of professors of sociology in England. Many of the people who were lecturers with us now have chairs.

However, I do find it sad that practically none of them took my approach further. Most of them regarded my way of thinking in long-term processes as lying outside the mainstream. And they were not mistaken, for it might have cost them their careers had they followed that approach. It was not at all fashionable in sociology to think in long-term processes.

Did you not want a career yourself?

I had no chance.

Why not?

Well, I consider myself fairly innovative as a sociologist, and all these innovations were really not acceptable at that time. Whenever I brought out an unusual idea in one of my annual lectures for my colleagues, it resulted in a very hostile argument with the younger generation.

Can you give an example?

Yes. One of these lectures was about personal pronouns. In it I said that as a sociologist one had to see things from the I-perspective, from the he/she-perspective, from the we-perspective and from the perspective of the third person plural – and all at the same time. I think that is a very good idea, but it was not at all well received; there is a very conservative streak in the English tradition.

The young people in the department probably regarded my innovative ideas as continental whimsy – though they were never tactless about them. But they did oppose me violently: hardly had I finished speaking than the battle started, and the whole seminar of my colleagues split into two hostile groups. I still remember how precisely that happened after my talk on Popper. I had attacked Popper, the great Popper, and that was naturally outrageous, coming from someone as little known as I was.

Popper is, moreover, one of the people of continental origin who have gained a firm footing in England. But to achieve that you doubtless have to be socially accepted by the English establishment. My sole contact in that direction was my friendship with C. P. Snow, which died out when I moved from London to Leicester. So I remained a person of the third rank. Perhaps I should add that I could put up with that without any deep traumatic effects, simply because of a certain inner toughness that I clearly possess. I never lost my belief in myself – the belief that I could achieve something relatively important. That belief has not been shaken by anything.

How is that?

Such a question cannot be answered. If you like, the security my parents gave me has always been with me.

I never threw in the sponge. The seminar with my colleagues was always the flashpoint; after each aggressive collision I came back the next year with something new, and now this or that piece is being published.

What I do not understand very well in all that is that I never planned my life. I went along like the rider on Lake Constance, without fear that I might fall through the ice. That is my basic feeling of life.

In the 1950s you were still an obscure figure. How did that change?

I was an outsider, and that only changed after I had left England. By the way, that step was not planned either – I did not decide one day to leave England, but was driven to it. I was invited as a visiting lecturer to Holland, I was invited to Germany, and so it gradually came about over many years that I lived in Germany more than in England. Finally, I gave up my house in Leicester.

But before that you lived in Ghana. When was that?

That must have been in 1962. Neustadt had contacts with Ghana and received an enquiry that they needed someone to take over the chair of sociology there for two or three years. He showed me the letter and I said, 'I'll do that.' Many of my friends thought me mad – after all, I was over sixty. But I have an immense curiosity about the unknown, so I went to Ghana.

How did you find it?

It was a magnificent experience, and through it I gained a deep liking for African culture.

I had always had the idea that our understanding of ancient Greek civilization, familiar to me from my humanist grammar school, is clouded because we do not realize that it was a relatively, I would not say primitive society, but one at a different level of development. We know, for instance, that the Greeks sacrificed bulls to their gods. For us that is literature, and on the Parthenon frieze we see the bull being led to the altar and sacrificed. But I wanted to see all that with my own eyes – the entrails spilling out, the blood spurting. I think that is an experience that we as civilized people, at our level of civilization, cannot reproduce; it is quite wrong of us to see these things only as literary metaphors.

I knew that in Ghana I would see magic acts, that I would be able to see animal sacrifices, *in vivo*, and I did in fact witness many things – experiences which have lost their colour in more developed societies. Naturally, this had to do with my theory of civilizing processes: the emotions were stronger and more direct.

Where did you live in Ghana?

On the campus, three-quarters of an hour's drive from the capital Accra. The university was arranged on the model of Oxford and Cambridge. People wore gowns, including the students; the professors ate at high table. I had my own car with a chauffeur and my own cook – all much more grand than I was used to in Leicester.

And where did you find the primitive culture you were looking for?

I would not use the word 'primitive'; I do not like it – 'simpler' is the right word, in the sense of 'less differentiated'.

In Ghana, with his cook (left) and chauffeur

Anyway... I did a lot of fieldwork with my students. I began to collect African art, and some of my students took me to visit their homes. There I learned how formalized and ritualized Ghanaian life is: the student stood behind his father's chair and behaved towards him almost like a servant. The old type of family authority is still very much in force in Ghana.

I also remember how I drove with my chauffeur through the jungle, until – deep in the jungle – we came to a village. There I saw for the first time what it means not to have any electric current; instead, there were hundreds of little flames from lamps that everyone carried. The people were still on the street, many things were happening in the street. 'A white man has come' – and then they surrounded me and asked me where I came from and where my wife was. That was always one of the first questions: 'Where have you left your wife? Where are your children?' That I did not have a wife they found incomprehensible, unimaginable.

I had one of my most memorable experiences in connection with the planning for a new power station on the Volta. The government had to prepare the inhabitants of a number of villages for the fact that their village was going to disappear in the big reservoir that was to be constructed. So I drove for almost a week from village to village with the head of the Ghanaian social services. He called together an assembly and explained to the people that the water would come and submerge their village and that the government would offer them other land. For me this situation, sometimes in the evening, in front of the chief's house, is unforgettable. Especially the intense arguments: what will happen to our ancestors? What will happen to the local gods? 'It will not happen,' they said, 'it cannot happen; it has never happened that the water has risen so far, we're too high up.' They could not understand what a power station was. Then the younger ones would say, 'All right, we'll just move.' They sat somewhat outside the circle – the inner circle being formed by the elders – and then the chief said: 'We shall not move!' Finally they agreed to a compromise: the government would give them three oxen that they could sacrifice to their ancestors, to pacify them, and would give them land that was just as fertile as their present land.

I must give credit to Nkrumah for sending a high government representative to the villages affected three years before the event, to prepare the people for it in long discussions.

What did you learn in Ghana about people and how they live together?

A very great deal. I would almost say it is an indispensable experience for someone like me. For instance, I was always of the opinion that the theory Freud left behind needed to be developed further. I thought that super-ego and ego formation in simpler societies would be different from ours, and this expectation was fully confirmed in Ghana.

I mean ... to restrain oneself, it is not enough simply to rely on one's own inner voice. People cannot survive if they do not impose self-restraint on themselves from an early age; but to do that they have to imagine that there are beings outside them which force them to do this or that. You see it everywhere if you go to such a country. Someone finds a strangely formed shell on the beach; he takes it with him and it becomes his personal fetish that he can ask to help him.

At that stage people live in far greater insecurity than we do. They are exposed to much greater dangers – illnesses, for example; the unexpected can happen to them much more than to us, and therefore they need protection that only gods or spirits can offer them. Thus a village can have fifty different gods, and in addition each household has its private gods. If one applies that to the personality structure, one has to conclude that the super-ego is constructed differently from ours, for all these gods and spirits are representatives of the super-ego.

The ego structure is much more easily breached by id impulses, and the boundary between fantasy and reality is not yet as sharp and stable as it is in us.

Much of what you say about Africa makes us think of children.

In that case you misunderstand how different it is... With regard to such an experience there are two attitudes, both of which I consider wrong. The first is – the usual colonialist attitude: that we are more rational, more advanced, and that they are simply more irrational, more childish. In a word, we are better. The second attitude, just as wrong, stresses how much better it is to give free rein to one's feelings and affects. It is indeed more colourful and easy to romanticize.

My own attitude is, I think, distinct from both. I see quite clearly that our way of life is only possible because our physical safety is incomparably greater than theirs. If we lived in similar insecurity, we too would seek the help of invisible powers. For people cannot survive if they are forever, at each moment, exposed to dangers they are unable to control.

Of course, I am drawing a one-sided picture here. Undoubtedly, there are many Ghanaians who are on the same intellectual level as we are – an upper class which is no less educated and self-restrained. But if I think of the mass of the people, I still see the little altars all over the houses before me. Or I remember how, on a field trip, I once asked a chief what we should do, and his advice was, 'Go first to the wise woman to gain her blessing.' We did that, three students and I. On the woman's table were fetishes, and she called on the little forest spirits to help us and our work.

Have such experiences caused you to change your view of religion?

No, not in the least. I have, and had then, neither the enlightened disdain for religion nor the romantic longing for it. I was always aware that under certain circumstances people can have a need of religion – but I do not have it.

Have you never had it?

Oh yes, as a child ... I think the First World War was the watershed. From all I saw there I came back with the realization that only human beings can help human beings, and only I can help myself.

Did you like African art before you went to Ghana?

No, I only came to appreciate it properly while I was there. In the course of time I had to learn to distinguish a good and genuine piece from one that was not.

Can you say anything more exact about what fascinated you in it?

Really the same thing as in Picasso. I'm sure you are aware of the link between African art and the development of art in Europe.

I have a very great affinity with contemporary painting and sculpture, and it was deepened when I discovered African art. That art expresses emotions far more strongly and directly than the traditional art of the nineteenth century or the Renaissance. And that fits in very well with my theory of civilizing processes; for in the Renaissance there was an enormous advance of civilization, expressed not least in the attempt to make paintings and sculptures as realistic as possible. In the twentieth century there was a reaction against that. One can also relate it to Freud: what happened in psychoanalysis – that on a new level a higher degree of affect expression could be permitted – is also seen in non-naturalistic art, which has a far greater resemblance to dream. African sculptures have the same quality. There are frightening masks and friendly masks, but they all give stronger expression, if you like, to the unconscious.

From Ghana you went back to Leicester.

Yes, that must have been in 1964. My post there was extended from year to year.

And then, slowly, success came.

I don't know. I have never seen it like that, hardly see it like that even today. Of course, I realize that by now I am highly respected in Germany and Holland ...

Let me put it like this: I am beginning to believe that I might be close to a stage where there is no longer a danger that what I have tried to do will be lost. But I am not absolutely sure that the danger is past. As you see, I still work very hard, and I am doing that with the conscious desire to bring about a situation in which my work will really become a part of the sociological tradition. I am still working very hard to reach that stage.

When did the first signs of a change of opinion become noticeable?

That I don't know. Actually, I still do not have the feeling that I am fully understood. There are so many themes in my writings that are not taken up. I do not yet have the feeling that my work is done.

The mere fact that the kind of theory I have tried to develop is different from what is traditionally regarded as theory, on the model of the physical sciences, creates enormous misunderstandings. But it is really my opinion that future models in the human sciences will lie more in the direction I have taken than in the direction of physical models. So I still hope I will have time to write more, to make myself better understood.

If you talk of success: I am naturally happy that I have received the Adorno Prize and the honorary doctorate at the University of Bielefeld. These are pleasing signs that I am getting a better hearing. All the same, I still have the fantasy that I have long had – that I am speaking into a telephone and the voice at the other end says, 'Could you speak louder, I can't hear you,' and then I start to shout, and the other voice keeps saying, 'Speak louder, I can't hear you.'

When did you first have that fantasy?

When I was first at Leicester, I think. Certainly, the voice at the other end says by now, 'I can hear you better now, a little better.' But still not very well. So I have to speak more clearly.

Does the voice in your fantasy speak German or English?

How could I distinguish? Nor do I think that I am fully understood in Germany. To put it differently: it is not the right question, whether it speaks English, German or Dutch ... I am a traveller! I am both or neither.

When did you return to Germany?

I cannot really say that I 'returned' to Germany, as it has been a gradual process. I had a visiting professorship in Münster, and then I went back to England. Then I had a visiting professorship for one year in Konstanz and again went back, so that gradually it turned into something permanent. I mean, I cannot give a day when I came back to Germany as the result of a definite decision. I slipped into it. It has always been like that in my life.

To be honest, the ZiF in Bielefeld has contributed more than anything else to my staying in Germany: the swimming pool, the forest, the intellectual atmosphere... I should always have liked to live in a college, but it was never offered to me in England.

Germany is, after all, something like your homeland, more than any other country.

That is difficult to say – culturally I am a German, yes.

In what way are you not a German?

Well... I am naturally very concerned about the potential for hostility towards foreigners; that is still high in Germany, even if it is not now directed against Jews but against the foreign workers. For that reason it is very good for me that I have a flat in Holland. Basically, I am a European.

Let me add that I never shared the idea that one can or should be identified with a single country. Clearly, you want to put me in this or that pigeonhole, but in my case that does not work. It gives me a certain satisfaction to be thought of as a German sociologist, but, of course, I am more than that.

If you were to ask someone about German sociology, about the four best-known German sociologists, he would give one of two answers – which you can actually hear: either that I am one of them or that I am a complete outsider. The second also applies, by the way, to American, English and French sociology. My ideas are recognized and adopted only in very small circles.

Do you see your work, your writings and ideas, as the most important part of yourself?

The word 'part' does not fit here: my work is the centre of what I feel to be meaningful in me. That was clear even in my schooldays – I wanted to do research, wanted to be a scholar of one kind or another and to be at a university. I knew that very early.

Have you liked working throughout your life?

That is expressed too simply, for it is hard work, learning to work. I made myself work; it was a hard struggle, not something that came of its own accord. I have had to struggle again and again, and I still have to.

I could wish very much that it was easier. I often have to rewrite the same thing eight times.

And what is the satisfaction you get from it?

That it turns out well. Then I know that it really is good, and that is the only thing that makes the effort worthwhile.

Yes, then I am content, and feel that I have not let myself be corrupted. I read in an English review recently – and it made me very angry – that I am perhaps the last representative of classical sociology, someone striving after the great synthesis, and so on. It made me angry because I would rather be the first one to open a new path. It shocks me again and again to find so many people losing heart, as if nothing was worth the trouble. There is so much to be done, and so many people are wasting their time with nonsense or being intellectually corrupted. My experience is that I am gradually seeing something new, something I did not know, and in that I am setting an example: one *can* do it, and it is worth the trouble.

I find it terrible – this lack of courage, this nihilism, this whining.

All your life you have had remarkable self-confidence.

I do not know if it is remarkable, but I have never doubted what I was doing.

It is remarkable if someone has the certainty that what he has to say is important.

Yes, that certainty was there even when I was swimming against the tide, against all those who had power. If I give myself credit for anything, it is that I have never been corrupted by any fashion. I never allowed myself to say anything because it was fashionable.

Of that I am really a little proud today – that I never gave way, although it was very difficult. It was always clear to me that the prevalent opinions were a fraud. I could have had a much easier life in England if I had accepted the prevailing ideas, but I did not get involved in compromises. I could not do that.

Perhaps it is just a matter of optimism, to believe in one's own ideas like that.

No, not a matter of optimism. It is the normal way of working for a scientist. One has a problem, and one day one knows: I have the solution. One has not thought it out – one *has* it. Take the example of Freud: where did he get his certainty from? He, too, swam against the stream, that is not so rare.

But you did have to wait a very long time before success came.

All right, I am very persistent. Of course. But Freud met with direct hostility, far more than I did.

It is easier to fight against that than silence.

Yes, I'm sure that is right. But I know that I see connections that many other people do not see, and therefore have a duty to say so.

Earlier it was taken far more for granted that one could really find something out by scientific work. Now such an

Norbert Elias, 1984 (Photo: Bert Nienhuis)

attitude seems unusual, as nihilism is so much in vogue; that used to be different. In this respect I am a fossil from an earlier age.

One has to bear in mind that for thousands of years religion was the centre of the human structure of meanings. Today for many people a great void has appeared in its place, and we offer them no substitute. In this situation I should like to show that one can live in a very meaningful way without religion. It may sound trite to sum it up in so few words, but I see it as one of our main tasks at present not to tell lies and not to create new father and mother figures in the sky. In that I see a further step in humanity's process of growing up, and nihilism is for me an attitude of people who do not want to grow up. I would like to allow myself a bit more leisure, but at the moment it seems to me very urgent to point out that these are the growing pains of humanity, that we shall one day manage without imaginary father and mother figures and still have to build up a meaningful life for ourselves as a society.

Described in that way, your work seems like the expression of a struggle for independence.

You cannot reduce it to a psychological problem. If that is what you mean, I must contradict you. We are talking about a social task. You misunderstand me completely if you take this immense social task as relating to an individual.

We are not 'independent'; no one is that, which is why I do not use the word. We are mutually dependent.

You have always placed your work above your 'personal' life. Did you never want to marry, have children?

Well, I noticed very early that the two do not go together: to do what I wanted to do and to be married. There is always a rivalry.

Was that a difficult decision?

I doubt whether the assumption behind your question is right. Such things always look as if they have been well thought out, but nothing was really thought about in this. Life takes a different course. Perhaps there are people who live like that and consciously decide on this or that path – I, at any rate, did not. For me it was not a decision.

But have you not sometimes regretted not having become a father?

No, not seriously. I mean, I have always very much liked teaching students, and you can, if you like, call that a substitute. Teaching has something fatherly about it.

We should like to come back to Germany once more. You must also have very negative feelings towards it. After all, the country has done very bad things to you.

Yes, certainly, but it does not befit me to repay anti-Semitism with something similar. I think it wrong and unjust to condemn a whole group of people. That was done so long with the Jews, and I am not prepared to do the same, no matter to whom. I will not condemn a whole people because of the Nazi period, still less after two or three generations.

But your mother was murdered, your career ruined.

And nevertheless, I do not say when I see a German: he is the murderer of my mother. It would be quite unrealistic.

Unrealistic, perhaps, but there is also something called hatred.

Well, how shall I put it? For instance, there is working here in the ZiF a former Nazi who at first behaved in a very odd way towards me – he tried to exaggerate in the opposite direction. I remained completely neutral, distanced. That deeply anti-German feeling, that you seem to have, is wrong.

You clearly feel it to be a moral obligation to go beyond it.

No, it is also a matter of feelings. I do not have these feelings, this feeling of hatred.

But you must surely have hated the National Socialists?

Yes, I hated them, but at the same time I had enough detachment to go to a Hitler rally. I was very curious about it.

At that time the worst had yet to happen.

That is true, and what remains is mourning... I simply cannot get rid of the picture of my mother in a gas chamber. I cannot get over it.

I still have the last letters my mother sent, through the Red Cross, when she was in the first concentration camp. Letters could still be sent from there. She was allowed to write ten words, no more.

My feeling is there, and it is very strong, even after forty years, I cannot get over it. But what should I do, what do you think I should do, if I meet that man? Should I go up to him and say, 'You are a scoundrel, you murdered my mother'?

I should like to write about the whole Nazi episode, but so much has yet to be clarified.

Do you still see yourself as a Jew?

Yes – that is, I *am* a Jew, a German Jew. In my whole make-up and also in my appearance. The way you put the question, it sounds as if I had a choice. But I can only answer: I have no choice, I am a Jew, no matter what I say or do.

That reminds me of a Jewish joke: if I am a Jew, I might as well be proud of it. But I don't think that. I think: I am not a Jew because I want to be, but because I am.

Are you a German in the same way?

A German Jew, that is correct. If I said simply, a German, that would not be quite correct.

Actually, I ought to say: I am a German Jew who has lived for thirty years in England. All that has gone into my make-up, and I am all that.

One last question: is there a place where you would most like to die?

No, the place does not matter; I should only like a painless death. When I become decrepit and of no use to anyone any more, I should like to disappear. But where that happens does not interest me.

And where would you most like to be buried?

That would no longer be 'I'.

But sometimes people have very exact wishes on that point.

Not I – I have not even thought about it. I am concerned with problems of the living, and I did actually write in one place: 'Dead people have no problems.'

Notes on a Lifetime
Norbert Elias

—◆—

What learning taught me

Many years ago, at a symposium of English sociologists, there
was a discussion on the weaknesses and strengths of contemporary sociology. A small episode from it has stayed vividly in
my mind. Barbara (later Baroness) Wootton, who was then
Professor of Sociology at Bedford College, University of London,
called out to the assembled sociologists in the course of a
somewhat embittered address: 'And none of you are proper
sociologists. Look around you. You and you and you' – she
pointed at some members of the audience – 'none of you has
ever studied sociology! You've all come in from somewhere else!'

At that time I was a fairly young sociologist in exile, without
a university post in England (though Barbara Wootton gave
me much help with lecture invitations to Bedford College,
among other things). At that lecture I stood up and pointed
out that, given the paltry number of chairs and departments
of sociology until recently – before the Second World War
there were two departments in the whole of England – it was
hardly surprising that the few older exponents of sociology had
not themselves studied sociology. First-generation sociologists,

I said, necessarily come from somewhere else. Such a situation could be observed in any newly institutionalized natural science. I hoped that I did not have to explain to sociologists the reasons for sociology's relatively late adoption as a normal academic discipline. Moreover, I added, it should by no means be taken for granted that it was a disadvantage to sociologists to have originally studied something other than sociology, such as economics or history, and to have acquired on their own initiative their knowledge of sociology and their understanding of the problems it set itself. It was characteristic of a false understanding of professional ethics, I asserted, to maintain that one had to have studied sociology, and nothing but sociology, to become a good sociologist. I sometimes had the impression that it was entirely beneficial to the richness and depth of the sociological imagination if its practitioners had studied something other than mere sociology. The professional academic ethic, which restricted the physicist to the study of a specialized physical field, the economist to the study of the economy and the historian to specific periods of history, was certainly adequate to a large number of applications of sociology in professional life, but not to the innovative, pioneering work of sociological research and teaching at universities; without that a discipline would ossify, and sociology, above all, needed it over and over again. This work required specialist knowledge – whether acquired in the normal course of study or in independent work – not only in the field of sociology but in those of other human sciences and maybe in this or that natural science, too; that is to say, knowledge going considerably beyond the standardized body of knowledge of professional sociology.

I don't know if this little harangue made me many friends among the English professional sociologists present at that time. I don't know whether these words increased my chances of resuming my interrupted university career in England. But at that time I lacked understanding of the wisdom of silence.

Among those I had summed up as 'first-generation sociologists', among those, that is, who had taken up sociology as their primary field of research and teaching after studying something else, probably as the result of a definite intellectual decision, there are many examples of the fertilizing of sociological work by the encompassing knowledge they brought to it. Here it may be enough to point to Max Weber. He was a lawyer by training. Some of his works, especially his *Soziologische Grundbegriffe* ('Basic concepts in sociology'), which is really a law-hook for sociologists, would be incomprehensible to anyone who did not take Weber's legal training into account. But, when he thought it necessary, Max Weber acquired a great deal of knowledge, particularly historical knowledge, through independent study. It might perhaps be worthwhile to trace out more exactly the experiences that induced Max Weber to turn himself into a sociologist. But whatever the reason for his going over to sociology, Max Weber was not a sociologist as a result of his study but by his own choice. The case was similar with many other sociologists of the 1920s. They were first-generation sociologists.

I am one of them myself. I had studied medicine and philosophy. Jaspers, in whose seminar I read my first major paper (on Thomas Mann and the *Zivilisationsliteraten*), told me, while out on a walk, something about Max Weber, whom he revered. But I cannot recall having read a single sociological book before completing my undergraduate course. When, at the end of the period of hyper-inflation in 1923, I went as a young 'Doctor' first to Heidelberg, where I had enjoyed being a student, I no longer attended Jaspers's seminar but Alfred Weber's. I got to know the sociology lecturer Dr Karl Mannheim, and went to his seminar too. Mannheim was only a few years older than I was, and we quickly became good friends. He was a first-generation sociologist, but as a former student of Lukács, and in connection with the intense politicization of his native country, he had a considerable knowledge of Marxist literature, which I entirely lacked. It was at that time, at about the age of twenty-eight or twenty-nine, that I began gradually to make myself familiar with the main works of sociology.

My own academic career had originally taken a quite different direction. The foundation had been laid at school. I

was lucky in the humanistic grammar school my parents sent
me to. In recollection, which may be selective and one-sided,
my years at the Johannes-Gymnasium in Breslau appear to me
as a time of great significance for my intellectual orientation.
In later years I heard of many schools which deadened rather
than stimulated their pupils' interest in the cultural riches of
their society. For that reason I have never ceased to look back
on my school with special gratitude. For reasons that have never
been clear to me, the Johannes-Gymnasium in Breslau was one
of the minority of grammar schools in the city at which Jewish
pupils hardly felt the pressure of concealed or open anti-Semitic
hostility among their teachers and fellow pupils. It was one of
the few grammar schools with a small number of Jewish teachers
in senior positions. The staff also included a number of men who
later made names for themselves as university teachers. Apart
from the mathematician Jüttner I remember with special vividness the classicist Julius Stenzel, who was my form teacher for a
time, and to whom I owe my interest in classical literature and
any understanding I have of it. Later, as a professor at Kiel
University, he became widely known among fellow scholars, as
are his works up to this day. I remember the little senior master
Dr Ries, to whom I owe the basis of my knowledge and love
of French language and literature, and Dr Krüger, who was
responsible, among other things, for organizing a special philosophy group among the members of my class. A number of
brilliant pupils belonged to it. I was friends with one or two of
them. We read Kant, and my later decision to study philosophy
as well as medicine was due in no small part to the stimulus
I gained through this group. I also vividly remember the doubts
I had about my own ability – doubts that arose from the
friendly rivalry within the group as to whether I should be able
to match the knowledge and brilliant intelligence of the leading
lights of the group.

It seems not unimportant to me to mention this basis of my
education here. It was still wholly imbued with the classical
pedagogical ideals of the German educated middle class. At its
centre were still the classics of Graeco-Roman antiquity and the

German classicists of the age of Schiller and Goethe. It is not
always easy to transport oneself back into the mental world
of the child one was more than seventy years ago, but as I search
back for memories, out of the semi-darkness an episode emerges
that was not a little characteristic of the individual and social
peculiarities of my childhood. At the age of thirteen, according
to Jewish custom, one was admitted to the ranks of the
grown-ups by means of a ritual in the synagogue followed by a
reception at one's parents' house. This reflected the conditions
of a much earlier stage of social development. The religious
customs remained unchanged. In my own society I was, at
thirteen, a schoolboy and not nearly an adult. Thinking back I
see myself at the time of this purely formal but unreal entry to
the adult world as a child, a clever little schoolboy. On the
occasion of this ritual a wide circle of relations and family
acquaintances would, I knew, give me presents. Most of them,
I was also aware, would go to a well-known Breslau bookshop
in search of suitable books. I therefore made a precautionary
visit to this bookshop a week in advance, asking them to advise
anyone enquiring about a suitable gift for the Elias's Bar-Mitzvah
that the young man wished for German classics in the edition
of the Bibliographisches Institut. This arrangement with the
bookshop would save us having to exchange numerous books.
And in the event I received, in addition to the collected works
of Schiller which I already had, those of Goethe, Heine, Mörike,
Eichendorff and other classics in the same edition.

Even now this early orientation of my education towards
classical German literature, expressed in my pride in owning
these books and my precocious immersion in these authors,
seems very revealing. It played a part in giving me broad and
deep access to human problems, even after I had gradually
realized the inadequacy of the idealist trend in philosophy, and
when, after I had gone over to sociology, I began to take an
increasingly critical view of the specific humanism of this tradition. It seems to me that my own sociological outlook evolved
from my fight against the unworldliness of this tradition and
its unmistakable after-effects in sociology. But this radical change

of view was the outcome of a relatively long process. A great number of experiences played their part in it. I am not sure if I am aware of all of them.

The war experience may have made its own contribution to this process. To be sure, it did not seriously undermine my desire to study philosophy, first kindled at school, when I came back from the front. But I was clearly undecided, since I resolved to study medicine as well as philosophy. How I managed this, how it was possible to follow two courses at once, is no longer quite clear to me. But I do realize that the two disciplines had a decisive influence on my intellectual outlook and particularly on my idea of the objectives of scholarly work. I continued my medical studies, with gradually waning interest, until the middle of my clinical semester. I then realized that I could not ride two horses at once. I decided to abandon medicine and concentrate on finishing my course in philosophy. But by then I had my intermediate preclinical examination behind me. In preparing for it, I had acquired quite a lot of knowledge of a number of scientific disciplines. Once again, I was lucky with my teachers. Anatomy is often felt to be a boring subject. Kallius knew how to make the study of the human body interesting, including the work in the dissection lab. I have kept my interest in the connections between muscles, bones, nerves and viscera until today, and I still cannot imagine how, as a sociologist, one could form an adequate idea of the human being without knowledge of this kind.

Later, I worked at one time on problems to do with laughing and smiling. They show in paradigmatic form, it seemed to me, how people are biologically attuned to each other, in a way that should not be overlooked even when one is primarily concerned with attunement acquired by learning, that is, social adaptation. Thanks to the knowledge I acquired during my years studying medicine, it seemed to me entirely natural not to separate the social aspects of human smiling and laughing from what might perhaps be called their biological aspects. I knew of the unique diversity of the musculature of the human face, observed how much more complex this musculature was than that of existing humanoid apes – how much more developed is, for example, the risorius muscle, which plays quite an important part in human laughter. From this side too, therefore, I was made aware that human beings are by nature attuned to living together with their own kind, to species-specific forms of communication which, partly if not exclusively, may be and must be activated and transformed by the assimilation of learned social patterns. By this piece of work I wanted to show, among other things, that the extraordinary individualization of the human face – especially when compared to the relative rigidity and far lower individual differentiation of animal faces – resulted partly from the special malleability and variety of the human facial muscles.

In contemporary debates on problems of the human body it is easily forgotten that the human face is a part of the human body. My fight against the still dominant image of the person as *homo clausus*, my so far largely vain attempt to convey to others the fundamental adaptation of human individuals to each other, their existential group-relatedness, is based in part on such physiological and anatomical knowledge. We often talk of a particular pattern of facial coordination as being the 'expression' of a feeling, as if the feeling were the cause and the pattern of movements of the facial muscles the effect. But that is the wrong way round; it is an example of the *homo clausus* mentality, which inclines us to think that anything directed outwardly, that is, especially towards other people – in this case the signal field of a face – is a kind of accidental accompaniment to the solitude of that person's inner existence. In reality the communicative signalling of feelings to other people is a primary feature of the human constitution. Facial signals and feelings are not related to each other in the same way as effect and cause. Both are originally aspects of one and the same human reaction. Feeling and expression belong primarily together. Only gradually, depending on the prevailing patterns of civilization, does a dividing wall become inserted between emotive excitement and gestures or movements of the facial muscles. Only gradually do children in more complex societies learn to laugh without feeling. And only then does it appear to people that their true self is imprisoned within themselves, cut off from any relationship to other people.

No doubt all this only became clear to me much later, but then it became one of the main pillars of my theory of civilization and of my sociological thinking in general. But whether I should have been able to elaborate clearly the new image of *homo non-clausus (sive sociologicus)*, whether I could later have developed it further without the knowledge I acquired during my study of medicine, is more than doubtful.

Without my realizing it fully at the time, my preclinical semesters, and especially my study of anatomy, had a profound influence on my basic ideas. Then as now I was interested above all else in the structure and functioning of the integrating human nervous system. During dissection I learned something about the structure and functioning of the human brain. Still quite young in my thought, I could not help comparing this knowledge of the nature of man that I gained in the dissecting room and then in the study of medicine itself, with the neo-Kantian image of man of my revered philosophy teacher Hönigswald (who, if I remember rightly, had also studied medicine). In philosophy, the postulate of an 'outer world' standing over against the 'inner world' of men and the sphere of ideas, of the transcendental constituents of an a priori reality, was taken for granted. As I dissected, I found inside the human head nothing except the extraordinarily complex structure of the brain. Although the riddle of its functioning was at that time far from solved, its basic structure was entirely attuned to the complementary nature of sense-perception and movement, to constant mediation between the 'inner' and 'outer' worlds, to a linking of orientation to locomotion in the encompassing world. The discrepancy between the philosophical, idealist image of man and the anatomical, physiological one unsettled me for many years. I became totally absorbed in this problem, ruminated on it endlessly, and only found a clear answer long after I had turned my attention to sociology. It took a great deal of time for me to move away from the dominant image of the human being hermetically sealed from the outside world, and to find my way to the opposed image of the individual fundamentally attuned to a world, to that which he or she is not, to other things and especially other people – a process closely linked to my decision to abandon the study of philosophy.

I remember having once hinted at such unresolved doubts to Hönigswald and being quickly put right by an allusion to the insufficiency of biologism and the validity of judgements, which was untouched by such taints. Only gradually did I realize that the concept of validity had no other function than the one Hönigswald used against me, in which it served as a component of a system of argumentation dedicated to defending the basic procedure of philosophy – the reduction of observable processes in the flow of time to something timeless, immobile and immune to change – against critical objections. Practising scientists have long known that Newton's laws have turned out to be partially rather than universally valid, and that a standard model of the universe that enjoys a consensus among physicists may be corrected in view of new observations or even abandoned altogether.

I realized only later that my study of medicine had been, at the least, one of the basic experiences that played a part in my decision to switch from philosophy to sociology. But even when I was giving my introductory lectures for sociology students in the 1960s, I sometimes had a sectioned model of the brain to hand. It seemed to me that as a sociology student one ought to have a rough idea of the structure of the human nervous system in order to be able to form the image of people that is essential to an understanding of social connections – an image of people as fundamentally attuned to a life among human beings, animals, plants and minerals.

Moreover, the study of basic medical sciences such as physiology and anatomy also taught me to mistrust the idea that the human being was a piece of matter. What emerged was that the human being was an enormously complicated organization of matter. The totality of the matter of which a person consists may still be present if the organization of that matter no longer functions properly or collapses altogether. But the organism then loses the ability to reconstitute itself, and we say that the person is dead.

It was in this connection that I was to gain my first clear ideas of what is meant by structure and function. I got to know which functions such entities as the central and peripheral nervous systems have within the organization of the human being, and how the structure of such a system matches its function. Social systems are in substance totally different from biological ones. Nevertheless, the experience I had in working on the latter helped me in no small way when the time came to begin to understand the former. It saved me from allowing the diagnosis of existing social structures to be corrupted by preconceived, political wish-images or fears, which indicate what the formations in question ought or ought not to be like, but not what they actually are like and how they actually function.

Neither as a pupil at school nor as a student had I learned to look on party political life in Germany with any eyes other than those of an interested but not too deeply involved spectator. Any intense commitment to a political party was alien to me. I do not believe that as a young person I knew why this was the case. Models of political commitment were virtually absent from the circles of my parents and relations. Even among my fellow pupils people with strong political allegiances were the exception. Naturally, we talked about the political events of the day; we discussed them sometimes with excitement, sometimes with a certain boredom. But most of the protagonists seemed to us to belong to a different world and one to which we personally had no access. Even my period of military service did little to change this. The Kaiser, the generals, even the commanding officers of the division to which I was attached as a member of a group of radio operators, were remote figures to the simple serviceman. My occasional participation in a soldiers' council, to which I was dispatched by my unit in 1918, probably because of my articulateness, only confirmed my feeling that politics was a lot of talk skirting around the issues, and not really my affair at all. And my study of medicine and philosophy deepened a commitment in me that went in other directions.

No matter how impressive were the models of scholarly commitment offered by some of my university teachers – men like Kallius and especially Hönigswald – their political allegiances remained entirely unknown to me.

It may be that my memory is playing tricks on me. Perhaps models of political commitment had long been at hand and I alone had been blind to them. To be sure, the onset of the great social crises had long ago driven me out of the ivory tower – more than three years of war and soldiering, the years in a factory in the depths of the great inflation and much else – but I did not find it possible to arm myself or harden myself enough to overlook the one-sidedness of views, the distortion of facts that you needed to become used to if you were to take a political stand and take any pleasure in the game of politics. All these big words, these half-truths, these unfulfillable promises!

When the hyper-inflation was brought under control, when my parents were again able to support themselves, I succeeded – for the first and last time in that period – in selling an article to a newspaper, the *Berliner Illustrierte*. There and then I gave in my notice in the sure knowledge that I could now earn my living by journalistic work and also that my parents, if it came to the worst, were again in a position to help me out, and I set off for Heidelberg in the vague hope of finding my entrée to an academic career.

My relationship with my revered teacher Richard Hönigswald, who was also my research supervisor, had ended in a quite genuine breach that would have been almost impossible to mend. In the course of my work on my doctoral dissertation I had gradually – in painful arguments with myself – arrived at the conviction that the whole idea of a priori truth did not hold water. I could no longer ignore the fact that all that Kant regarded as timeless and as given prior to all experience, whether it be the idea of causal connections or of time or of natural and moral laws, together with the words that went with them, had to be learned from other people in order to be present in the consciousness of the individual human being. As acquired knowledge they therefore formed part of a person's store of experiences. And as this now seemed to me irrefutable, I wrote as much in my dissertation. Hönigswald pronounced it downright wrong. Without giving any reasons that I found convincing, he instructed me to change my argument. He could not accept it as it was. We both stood by our opinions – as I have done up to this day – until I had to admit that his power potential was greater than mine. I deleted the most explicit passages, toned down a few others, sent him the diminished product, which he accepted without comment, and I was thus made a D.Phil. of Breslau University. The manuscript of my dissertation has been lost. In view of the difficult times I only had to print a short excerpt at that time.[1] But it seemed pointless to ask Hönigswald to supervise my subsequent *Habilitation* thesis which would qualify me as a lecturer.

Incidentally, this wrangle has not in the least diminished either my high regard for the man or my gratitude for what he taught me. He was authoritarian like many German professors of his generation, would not put up with any nonsense and had little patience with fools and metaphysicians. What he perceived as philosophical speculation, including Husserl's phenomenology, he rejected. Heidegger and existentialism in general he thought not worth discussing, and he had difficulty concealing his contempt for such inexact modes of thinking. From Hönigswald (and from my father) I learned how to think. That means more than these brief words can express. I owe to him in particular, if not only to him, a conscience that does not allow me to let though any slovenliness of thought, affectations, poses, false fronts, in short, little of anything that is not germane to the question. I admit, of course, that my conscience sometimes falls asleep. He was just as implacable towards himself. Among the neo-Kantians of his time he was undoubtedly one of the most original. When I say that I learned how to think from him, I mean, to think productively; I mean he taught me, through his example, to trust thinking. He gave me the confidence that through reflection one may discover something new and something certain. The complementary activity of observing, the strategy of empirical work, I then had more or less to teach myself, when my switch to sociology made it necessary, although the experiences of the war and the postwar years, and my medical studies, probably helped.

Thus armed against dubious modes of thought, I went to Heidelberg. From my time there as a student I had the best memories of that lively little town. And I could see more clearly than when I had been there earlier where I was actually trying to go, what I wanted to accomplish with my life. I had the example of my university teachers before me. My wishes had long been drawn in this direction, and now I had gained the confidence that I could do it: teach and pursue research. I knew that I was a good teacher; among my fellow students I had got a reputation for being able to explain complicated subjects in a simple way. I enjoyed teaching. As regards research, I had little more than my dissertation as evidence of my ability. And that had been a difficult task. I had confidence in my intellectual capabilities, and I wasn't lacking in ideas. But the concentrated intellectual work demanded by the dissertation had been very difficult. I only realized later that about 90 per cent of all young people have difficulty writing their first major piece of research; and sometimes the second and third or even the tenth, for that matter. I could have wished someone had told me so at the time. You think, of course, 'I am the only one who has such difficulty in writing my dissertation (or whatever it might be); everyone else finds it quite easy.' But that's not how it is. So I say it now. The difficulties are perfectly normal. One just has to keep going. I knew that I was lucky in myself. I never found the work very easy, but I had staying power, I stuck at it.

In Heidelberg I was quite quickly drawn into the vortex of academic events. Heidelberg at that time was a preindustrial university town in the old style, which means that the university dominated the town. A considerable proportion of its inhabitants made a living from the university, even if indirectly. Students were a prominent factor in the everyday scene. But Germany's transformation from an imperial realm into a republic had brought with it definitive changes. Before 1918 students' associations, with their colourful caps, their ribbons and canes, their carefully cultivated scars and their duels, and the rich trappings of their other ritualized formalities, had played the leading part. Now the 'free students' (as they were still called), that is, young men and women who did not belong to any of the students' associations, who formed their own barely organized circles and were far more informal in their manners and modes of living, played a far more influential, almost the leading role, in the life of the city and, above all, in the university's intellectual life. At the time when I was in Heidelberg, from 1924 to 1929–30, the city had great intel-·lectual vitality, a wealth of distinguished figures among the teaching staff and an academic standard that placed high demands on the individual student, at least in the circles I was in contact with.

These circles, in particular, were those of the sociologists. That, too, was one of Heidelberg's special features at that time. At that university sociology enjoyed a high status. Memories of Max Weber played a big part in this. Alfred Weber not only tended the heritage, but gave the subject a new impetus in his own way. And Max Weber's widow, Marianne, played an important part as trustee of the tradition, in a way that I shall come back to. Certainly, at that time Max Weber and his work had not yet attained the international stature they were to enjoy later. But as far as the status of sociology in Germany was concerned, and especially, of course, in Heidelberg, the emergence of an exemplary sociologist with a resonance far beyond his own discipline was of the utmost importance. Nor did he, for those living at the time, stand out from the representative group of sociologists of the 1920s to the same extent as it may seem in retrospect, as a result of the tacit selection process carried on by later generations. Many figures among the old guard, whose works were hardly less highly regarded, men like Tönnies, Sombart, Scheler and Franz Oppenheimer, were still alive. The works of Troeltsch, like those of Simmel, were part of the accepted intellectual furniture of sociology which, impelled by the Heidelberg atmosphere, I now made my own. And in the background there stood, as always, taciturnly eloquent, the colossal figure of Karl Marx.

Whatever one might say, again and again the ebb and flow of sociological debate swirled largely around him. The argument either for or against Marx's theory of society, with its grand-children and great-grandchildren, played a permanent part, overtly and far more often covertly, in the sociology of ad-vanced industrial societies at that time. But it would be wrong to mention this fact without adding that this role was closely bound up with the persistent tension between the proletariat and the employers, and between the corresponding political parties, within this society itself.

When at the start of the 1920s I had briefly studied in Heidel-berg, I lived among the philosophy students. I joined in the seminars of the venerable Rickert, among others. And the rela-tively young Jaspers encouraged me to follow my own inclina-tion and make the controversy between Thomas Mann and the *Zivilisationsliteraten* (writers in the service of western rationalist culture) – as he contemptuously called them – the subject of an extended seminar paper. But when, in 1924, I arrived for a second time in Heidelberg, adorned with my doctorate and on the lookout for chances of 'habilitating', in order that I might graduate to the ranks of lecturers, my interest had changed direction. I went to lectures and seminars held by sociologists. And the students, male and female, whom I got to know there were incomparably more politicized than the philosophy students. There was, moreover, a curious division among them. To Alfred Weber, whose assistant at that time, if I remember rightly, was Arnold Bergsträsser, went students of all political hues, includ-ing those of the extreme right – though with the exception, if I am not mistaken, of those of the far left. Whereas those of the extreme right were absent from the seminar of the young *Privatdozent* Dr Karl Mannheim. There the spectrum of poli-tical nuances among students ranged from the Communists through sympathizers of the Independent Socialists to young Social Democrats and Democrats. In these circles I soon found a footing, although I made no secret of the fact that I was of no party and intended to stay that way.

I quickly made friends with Mannheim, and as I was older than his students and only a few years younger than he was himself, and as I also had far more contacts among students than he had, I slipped unawares into the role of his unofficial assistant. When, at the end of the 1920s, not long after the publication of *Ideology and Utopia*, he was appointed to the chair of sociology at Frankfurt-am-Main, he asked me if I would go with him as his official assistant. I agreed, on the condition that I could take my *Habilitation* as soon as possible. Mannheim told me he was willing to let me obtain this qualification under him provided I committed myself to work first for three years as an assistant to him. I had an opening for *Habilitation* under Alfred Weber too, but I was fourth on his list of candidates. On Mannheim's I was first. So I accepted his offer of a three-year wait before qualifying as a university teacher. That was in 1930. Three years later Hitler came to power. I just managed to get through the *Habilitation* formalities (apart from the inaugural lecture), but it did me little good. I went into exile, too old to start studying again, too young for a professorship.

But when I was slowly finding my feet in Heidelberg in 1924, we had hardly an inkling of all that. Mannheim's chair at Frankfurt was still in the far distance. Alfred Weber's consenting to consider me as a candidate for *Habilitation* pleased me. But that could still take a long time. Mannheim explained to me that to make sure of things it would probably be essential and certainly useful to get Marianne Weber's agreement to my plans. She kept a kind of salon, and it was advisable for a young sociologist aspiring to a university career at Heidelberg to make an appearance there. Soon afterwards I received an invitation to Marianne Weber's house. There, at regular intervals, a part of the Heidelberg academic elite gathered – men like Ernst Robert Curtius, women like Frau Jaffé, who after her husband's death lived with Alfred Weber.

Marianne Weber was an impressive woman, and made the impression on me of a doughty owner of a large intellectual estate, with her feet planted firmly on the ground, well able to manage her affairs and guarding what was hers. If you were one of her group you could rely on her. I don't know if I was right, but I had the idea that without this strong woman Max Weber would not have had the staying power to achieve all that he did. You have to imagine the dreadful strain, the enormous concentration needed to write something like *Economy and Society*. You can then understand his breakdown and what her help meant to him at that time, and also the fact that she dominated him, taking him – and after his death his legacy – into her possession. In her dealings with strangers she was courteous, reserved, keeping her distance. There was no doubt that at that time she was part of Heidelberg's intellectual landscape and, no less than her brother-in-law Alfred, someone to be reckoned with in the world of Heidelberg sociology. It was said that she had considerable influence on Alfred Weber, particularly with regard to young *Habilitation* candidates. Her veto could be fatal. But if you were a young person moving about in the handsome, slightly old-fashioned rooms of the Weber house, and especially on the large balcony with a view over the Neckar, you had little chance of finding out what really went on in this circle.

One day, after a few friendly words, she invited me to give a reading at one of her afternoons. That was normal. I had expected it, although the invitation might not have come. That it did come was a good sign. A date was agreed, and three weeks later, on the balcony if I remember rightly, I gave my little lecture on the sociology of Gothic architecture. I had often set off with a group of hikers and a copy of Dehio in my rucksack, making our way from one great cathedral to the next, and had long since discarded the romanticized view of the cathedrals as striving up towards heaven, knowing that the mighty buildings had jutted, far more than the Sundays-only churches of our day, into the everyday lives of the citizens. The booths of the small traders clung to their walls. The noise from the market came through the open doors and mingled with the sounds of the Mass. The high roofs, emblems of the rival cities with their unbridled pride – each of them wanting the tallest spire – and the unspeakable poverty, crying to heaven. I spoke of the differences in the structures of the German and French societies and their reflections in the structures of their cathedrals. At the end there was polite applause and kind words. A small step on the way to a university career. In the salon of the widow of Max Weber – I had not been cast out.

Meanwhile, I had talked with Alfred Weber about the subject of a *Habilitation* thesis. He told me I would have to wait four or five years. Several young people were ahead of me in the queue. But he seemed to like my proposed subject: the importance of Florentine society and culture for the rise of science. The plan, inspired by Olschki's *Geschichte der italienischen Literatur* ('History of Italian literature'), did, however, offer a number of difficulties. I could just read Italian if I had to, but that was all.

In the meantime I had to contend with other problems. The extraordinary politicization of the whole of the intellectual life I came into contact with in Heidelberg was a special challenge. This politicization of the intellectuals was undoubtedly a reflection of the power struggles going on between the different parties and, increasingly, between extraparliamentary paramilitary organizations in society at large. But it was a peculiarly esoteric reflection. While the power struggles outside grew increasingly brutal, their reflection among social scientists, particularly sociologists and economists, kept their civilized form. Among the students and lecturers there were right-wing social scientists and left-wing social scientists. The former included sociologists associated with Hans Freyer, who later took a leading role in the organization of German sociology under Hitler, while trying from time to time to mitigate some of the harshness of National Socialism. Another focal point for the social scientists of the right was the journal *Die Tat*. The group around this journal became known as the '*Tat* circle'. Whereas the young left-wing academics based themselves intellectually and organizationally on the working class, for some parts of the young academic right, centring primarily on the members of the

'*Tat* circle', the white-collar workers took on a similar importance. Those who sympathized with this circle found reason for hope in the growing numerical strength of the white-collar stratum, which, they hoped, might soon be backed up by a corresponding organizational strength. This suggested to them that the evolution of society itself might create in the growing class consciousness of white-collar workers a counterweight able to hold its own with the mass movement and class consciousness of the working class.

There was a scattering of National Socialists among the young academics of the right. One of them was an assistant of Alfred Weber. As a liberal Alfred Weber was, by his deeply rooted convictions and his principles (if not always by his passionate temperament, which showed through the conscious controls), a tolerant man. He would also have taken on a Communist as an assistant, if the question had arisen. No matter what it cost him in terms of his personal preferences, the principle of tolerance demanded it of him, and he took this principle seriously. The fact that he accepted a Jew among his *Habilitation* candidates reflected the same attitude. This conviction also required him to have a National Socialist as an assistant. At that time no one knew what fruits the seed would bear, and when they appeared he opposed them bravely and in vain. Before that, in the late 1920s, he made it his task as a liberal professor to show an exemplary tolerance. The young National Socialist deserved his post as assistant on merit, just as the Jew Elias deserved his acceptance as a *Habilitation* candidate. So why not?

People said that Alfred Weber felt overshadowed by his great brother. It is likely that he did suffer from that nightmare, but I have no proof of it. One could not, and cannot, help comparing the brothers. Both were members of a generation where you could allow yourself to set up as your main hypothesis in your books whatever happened to fit in with your wishes and ideals. But Max Weber had a conscience that drove him to test what it was he desired very strictly, whether in terms of its demonstrability by empirical evidence, or in terms of the intrinsic logic of the arguments on which it was based. Also,

Max Weber was really a passionate man, but he hardly ever allowed his passions to be manifested openly in what he wrote. You have to look very closely to discern where they guided his pen.

If a Mohammadan were to write a book in which he suggested that the spirit of Islam was responsible for the rise of the modern world, he might have difficulty in setting out his thesis in such a way that it did not give rise to the suspicion that he was writing *pro domo*. Max Weber's sober, logical exposition of a similar hypothesis, underpinned with empirical proof, seemed largely to rule out such suspicions. The same applies to the function of his work as a sketch of a counter-hypothesis to the Marxian concept of history, that is, his thesis that religion as such could give a stimulus to economic development, rather than that economics merely drove forward the development of religion. In this respect, too, Max Weber's manner of exposition was so detached, so free of any sign of partisanship, that although the popular impact of the work as a bourgeois counterblast to the materialist concept of history was in no way diminished, even a close reading could only occasionally, in conjunction with a wide-ranging study, bring to light proofs of such ideological bias. This ambivalence was not intentional. What I have tried to say here is not meant to call Weber's intellectual integrity into doubt. It is rather, as we shall see, an expression of a problem of modern sociology that began to interest me in Heidelberg. This problem was later reflected in my concern, never quite abandoned, with the problem of involvement and detachment.[2]

In the course of my work for my doctorate I had already realized that it was not possible to grasp in thought the manifold aspects of the human world and the connections between them by starting from the traditional 'subject of knowledge', as if a person could actually become a person at all without living with other people and learning from them. I had undoubtedly come to this realization through my experience of social life itself, for example, in the war; book-learning was certainly not central to it. I had long understood that in thinking about human affairs one had to take *people* rather than *the person* as one's starting point – that is, human pluralities, groups of people and the societies formed by many people together. Even in my dissertation,[3] which, in view of the circumstances, was still written in a wholly philosophical style, with a consequent tendency to see human history as if it were the mental product of individual people, I had stated unambiguously that the traditional concept of the 'individual' needed to be developed further. And it seems to me that this task of releasing the individual from intellectual isolation and inserting him/her, even in our conceptual model, into the chain of generations, the order of succession, has continued to be one of the central obligations of sociology.

In the course of my experiences of the war and inflation I too had become more aware not only of the relative powerlessness of the individual in the social structure, but also of the peculiarly esoteric character of the basic assumptions of philosophy, one of which was the idea of the omnipotence of thought. Even then, in my work on the place of the individual in history, I was already on the track of this problem of the diachronic order of succession, that is, of long-term social processes as an order *sui generis*. But to begin with the only tools I had at my disposal to come to grips with such processes were those of philosophy. I could only grasp them conceptually, as if these sociohistorical processes were mental processes, a sequence of reasons with consequences[4] that gave rise to further reasons for new consequences, and so on. But what I was dealing with in that form in 1922–4 was clearly – as it still is today – the peculiar order of long-term processes and their difference from the lawlike order of physical nature, as a kind of framework for human history.

Alfred Weber and Karl Mannheim (1)

Engrossed with such problems, I made my second entry to Heidelberg. And I found that the problems then exercising the minds of social scientists there were indeed closely related to my own. There, too, people were wondering about the peculiar order of what is conventionally called history. The central point at issue was not so much what I would now perhaps call the structureless history of historians, but rather the structured history of sociologists, which in the nineteenth century had found paradigmatic expression in the works of Marx and Comte, and the study of which had been given new impetus and vitality in Germany, mainly by the work of Max Weber.

Following on from the work of his brother, but doing so in his own way, Alfred Weber, as I soon discovered, was working on sociological problems of this kind. He was interested above all in the peculiarity of 'culture' as a vital aspect of every human society and its evolution. One of his concerns was to show how culture as a social formation cannot be reduced to economic factors or explained by economic interests. He started out from the idea that culture was created by human beings and therefore had always to be understood partly with regard to the social relationships of human beings. But the developmental pattern of culture, of such human formations as art or religion – as seen by Alfred Weber, if I remember rightly – differed in a very characteristic manner from the developmental pattern of such utilitarian human formations as economics, technology and science. In the realm of the latter there was progress, whether in a straight line or dialectical, and there were certainly also regressive movements. But the concepts of progress and regression could not really be applied to art or religion or, therefore, to culture. In his eyes the latter were founded solely on themselves, as self-sufficient formations in which – speaking symbolically – the spirit of an age or the soul of a people manifested itself.

I soon realized that in his work on the sociology of culture Alfred Weber was taking further an earlier tradition which had as one of its offshoots the antithetical use of the two concepts, 'culture' (*Kultur*) and 'civilization' (*Zivilisation*). I had already come across it during my first stay in Heidelberg, when I was working on my seminar paper for Jaspers. In his book *Betrachtungen eines Unpolitischen* ('Reflections of a non-political man')

Thomas Mann wrote at length on the opposition between 'culture' and 'civilization' in this sense. In this conceptual antithesis a very deeply rooted, specifically German version of intellectual and political conservatism found expression – a kind of conservatism which, as I have shown elsewhere,[5] can only be understood in the context of the special development of German society. Thomas Mann was not entirely wrong in taking Eichendorff's 'Taugenichts' ('Good-for-nothing') – the young singer of folksong-like poems who travels around the country, wholly aloof from politics, guided solely by his inner feelings and devoid of outward purposes – as a kind of symbolic embodiment of what the word culture meant for him. To this character, whom he admired, Mann had counterposed a figure he hated, that of the *Zivilisationsliterat*, a composite image based on his brother Heinrich Mann as well as Kurt Hiller and other left-wing intellectuals, who had criticized the existing order even during the 1914–18 war and upheld such ideals of western civilization as rationality, humanity and parliamentary democracy.

Now, in the work of Alfred Weber, I came across a concept of culture which, although well supported by factual arguments, at the same time had the significance of an emotive symbol and, as such, stood in the same tradition as Thomas Mann's concept of culture. One would have needed prophetic powers to have foreseen that the widely ramifying heritage of the German anti-civilizational tradition would also give rise to such a thing as National Socialism. And the mere idea that Alfred Weber's name could be mentioned in the same breath as that of the Hitler movement needs to be preemptively refuted. Alfred Weber was one of the people of integrity who had the courage to hold out against the tide when the National Socialist movement swamped Heidelberg University. The fact that he found the utilitarian, rationalist humanists of the left fundamentally abhorrent in no way permitted him to debase his own standard of civilization by a 'pact with the barbarians'.

Human beings are ambivalent creatures; unlike books, they cannot be expected to be free from contradictions. Like his brother Max, Alfred Weber was really a passionate man. But in him a no less passionate prejudice was in far more open conflict with his humane tolerance, his liberal rationalism; it permeated his scholarly work far more directly and overtly. Unlike Max Weber, who would never have permitted it (with great benefit to the longevity of his works), he allowed a kind of personal metaphysics to infuse and influence his factual investigations. Here we find once more the time-honoured contrast between a group of human products which were conceptualized as entirely self-sufficient and hence purposeless, and another consisting of products which were purposeful and useful – a contrast which is given a value emphasis characteristic of a specifically German tradition. The factual distinction went hand in hand with an unambiguous value distinction which represented culture as a group of products distinguished by their especially high value and civilization as a group of products of far lower value.

It was by no means the case that I saw through this state of affairs straight away. But my attention to it had been sharpened to some extent by my study of the quarrel between Thomas and Heinrich Mann. At first I failed to perceive how passionately something that might have been portrayed in the Diltheyan manner simply as an impersonal intellectual trend, a connection existing purely in the history of ideas, was manifesting itself here in the person of a human being as a highly individual, totally sincere and deeply felt conviction.

Nor did I notice straight away that the liberal-conservative sociologist of culture, the proponent of spiritual values, did not find his antagonist, the spokesman of all that he regarded as pertaining to a utilitarian and therefore shallow ideal of humanity, only among the relatively anonymous left-wing factions and movements in the wider world. He found his adversary right in Heidelberg itself, in the person of another sociologist, Karl Mannheim.

In 1924, when I arrived in Heidelberg, Karl Mannheim was thirty. In these Heidelberg years, spurred on by the clear goal of a chair in sociology, he was at the peak of his productivity.

In these years he wrote *Ideology and Utopia* and a large number of essays, including the lecture on 'Competition as a cultural phenomenon'. He was a brilliant thinker and a formidable debater. His ambition – competition in the intellectual sphere was a very personal problem of his – went hand in hand with a certain innocence of outlook. He seemed unaware himself of how ruthless he could be in the struggle with competitors. He knew that he was better than the next man, that he deserved the prize he was competing for. He took it for granted. He meant no harm by crushing his rivals. He was sure that he deserved the prize.

And in fact he usually was better. That was one of the reasons why his ambition was not unpleasant. He deserved success. He can hardly be blamed for having had to fight a second time for a university chair, in England, during his second exile – Germany was the first. Few people have succeeded in winning a full professorship twice over, as exiles in a foreign country with a language they had not entirely mastered. Mannheim performed this feat twice while fleeing from dictators: first in Germany, having been expelled by Horthy from Hungary; then a second time in England, fleeing from Hitler. Mannheim's achievement might perhaps have been greater had his career been less important to him. But that is a matter on which one cannot pass judgement.

Mannheim, as is known, took up the Marxian thesis that thought not only may be but must be influenced by interests, and developed it further in a particular direction. For Marx this proposition was closely linked to the concept of class struggle. And in his version it had no relativizing undertones, since it states, in effect, that only oppressing and exploiting classes have to distort or conceal social reality through forms of thinking that express their economic interests. Anyone thinking from the standpoint of the oppressed, and especially from that of the industrial proletariat, does not need to use thought ideologically to obscure and distort social conditions. As a Marxist, therefore – so this argument runs – one is able to think and speak about society in a manner faithful to reality or, in other words, scientifically. In a weak moment, Marx formulated this factual relationship by saying that being determines consciousness. This idea was reflected in the linguistic usage of Mannheim and his contemporaries. They spoke of the 'being-dependence' (*Seinsgebundenheit*) of thought.

The Marxian formulation conjures up the idea of an ontological dualism, with a social existence of humans devoid of consciousness on one hand and, on the other, a consciousness passively tossed about by this consciousness-less social 'being', like a cork on the waves. In the same way Mannheim's formulation of thought as being-dependent suggests the dualistic idea of a quite thought-free social 'being' to which thought is added as something subsequent and secondary. And here too a simple billiard-ball causality is implied: changes in thought-free being as the cause are responsible for changes in thought as their effect. That ideas purporting to be correct turn out on closer inspection to be means used by certain groups for propaganda in their struggle against other groups can be observed often enough. And if such functions of ideas are examined systematically, they yield a genuine sociological problem of major importance.

Mannheim's treatment of this important problem, like Marx's, suffers from having been formulated without regard for the fact that consciousness and thought are themselves constituents of human society. The whole functioning of social life among human beings is influenced by the nature of their conscious perception of this social life, by what they think and the way they think. The dualistic thesis of a being alien to consciousness and a consciousness alien to being is a fiction. But Mannheim stood by this fiction. He went beyond Marx to the extent of postulating that it was not only the thought of one's adversary that should be perceived as a position-related ideology, so that its claim to truth was destroyed. Nor was it enough to point to the partial determination of certain elements of consciousness. Rather, the totality of consciousness should be shown to be an expression of a specific 'existential situation', that is to say, as tied to a position. Indeed, it was not only the totality of the

NOTES ON A LIFETIME

consciousness of other opposing groups or people that should be viewed in this way but also the totality of one's own consciousness. He thus found himself caught in a trap somewhat similar to the famous one of the Cretan, as told by the ancient philosophers. A philosopher from Crete said: all Cretans are liars. As he was himself a Cretan the statement has to be taken as a lie. But if it is a lie that all Cretans lie, then the statement must be true. But if it is true that all Cretans lie, then this statement too is a lie, and so on. If all statements are being-dependent ideologies, then this statement too is a being-dependent ideology. Whoever advocates this opinion can accordingly produce nothing other than ideology. Why, then, take the trouble to engage in any research, since every statement is tied to a standpoint and is in this sense ideology?

Mannheim had the ability to expound his views with great brilliance and vigour. In addition, what he had to say was really of great importance, and people were by no means wrong to see it as revolutionary. A long, powerful and respected tradition made the thoughts of individual people, their 'ideas', seem like autonomous, wholly self-sufficient and, as it were, free-floating products. The current concepts themselves, such as 'mind', 'ideas', 'thoughts', gave credence to this notion, and large and highly respected branches of knowledge, such as the humanities and the history of ideas, were clearly designed to investigate such free-floating mental formations. Of course, Marx and Engels had begun the process of unmasking individual ideas as the possible ideology of ruling classes. But now Mannheim came along and seemed at first sight to be in some respects far more radical than Marx. What he postulated basically was that all ideas, and thus thinking altogether, including the ideas of Marx and, to be consistent, his own as well, should be understood – to use his own language, which was really still that of Marx – as 'being-dependent', as expressions of a standpoint within the struggles between social parties which narrows one's view. This meant radically deposing the self-sufficiency of 'mind', and totally unmasking ideas as expressions of position-related partisanship.

If this position was thought through to its end, it really meant the total ruin of all the intellectual efforts of human beings. Mannheim himself drew back from this logical conclusion of his own argument. To escape the despair of total and purely destructive relativism, he coined the concept of relationism to counteract its poison. Each person, this idea roughly implied, is certainly 'being-dependent' in their thought. Other people, especially people with a different class standpoint, have a different partial perspective on the world. Might one not perhaps say that 'truth' was the totality of these partial perspectives?

Mannheim experimented with a number of ideas by means of which he sought to climb back out of the trap of relativism into which he had fallen. This, his relationism or perspectivism, was one of his safety ropes. How useful it was is not easy to say, since the concept of ideology always carries an implication of a certain distortion through interests, whereas the concept of perspective suggests a partially correct view. Where does this partial correctness come from, if all thought is ideology? Another safety rope that Mannheim experimented with was the idea that groups of intellectuals, who are not tied into the situation of class conflict as industrial employers and workers, are in their attitudes perhaps less closely bound to class ideologies, and in their perspective on society perhaps less directly influenced by economic interests, than the economic classes.

The quandary Mannheim found himself in was undoubtedly made no easier by the fact that his own political sympathies lay with the moderate left and that a *Privatdozent*'s hopes of gaining one of the few chairs of sociology in the first German republic could hardly be fulfilled without the active help of an influential party organization. I have often wondered whether the special place Mannheim gave utopia outside the ideologies, despite the fact that it ultimately has the character of an ideology and despite his own concept of total ideology, might have resulted from an involuntary attempt on his part to rescue socialism from relativization as ideology.

Alfred Weber and Karl Mannheim (2)

In my uneasiness about the unscientific nature of sociological theories, Mannheim's concept of ideology was undoubtedly a great help to me. In this there was a clear convergence between my feelings and my intellectual interest. I realized only gradually that there were distinctions to be made. Mannheim saw very clearly the connection between the views on society of certain people and groups and the social position of these people in society, especially as regards their interests. And in his study on conservative thought[6] he provided an exemplary analysis of ideologies. But he stopped short at this point. He did not go beyond a critical unmasking of other people's thought structures as ideologies, and probably did not want to go beyond it. He was content to relativize and disintegrate them. For me, criticism of ideology was only a means to an end, a step on the way to a theory of society that would take account of the fact that reality-revealing as well as reality-concealing knowledge can be observed. A doctor's knowledge of the human body, that can heal, is not ideology. Why should one not be in a position to produce non-ideological knowledge of human society?

Working together with Mannheim was always a pleasure, in Heidelberg as later in Frankfurt. In Heidelberg he was, as I have said, at the peak of his intellectual productivity. He not only had immense intelligence but great skill in debate; the destructive pungency of his attacks could often conceal the high level of abstraction at which his mind worked. All this drew intelligent students to him, including some female ones, although they were very much in a minority in Heidelberg.

As a *Privatdozent* Mannheim was clearly subordinate in power and standing to Alfred Weber, the full professor. But a large number of people saw in him the coming man of Heidelberg sociology. Although I attended both Alfred Weber's and Mannheim's seminars, at first I completely failed to notice the smouldering, underground rivalry between the two men. At that time the dealings between people in Heidelberg university circles were moderate in tone. In their comments on each other, as far as I heard them, both Weber and Mannheim were extremely cautious.

It was therefore all the more surprising when the antagonism between the two men suddenly broke out so openly. The occasion when this happened was the Sixth Congress of German Sociologists in Zurich. It was somewhat unusual for a *Privatdozent* to be called on to read one of the main papers on such an occasion. I myself was not very well versed in such matters of etiquette. It was still generally taken for granted that the speakers at such events would appear in strict hierarchical order, first the highest ranking full professors, especially Privy Counsellors such as Alfred Weber and Sombart, then the younger professors, who usually were not so well known, then the *Privatdozenten*, and, finally, young Ph.D. holders like myself who were mostly unofficially waiting for promotion to *Privatdozent* status were allowed to contribute something to the discussion if they so desired. It was thus a sign of the exceptional reputation Mannheim had made for himself that he was chosen to give one of the main lectures at the sociologists' congress.

The point under discussion was one of his central concerns, the problem of social competition. The doyen of German sociology, Leopold von Wiese, then editor of the *Kölner Zeitschrift*, gave the first lecture on this subject, Mannheim the second under the title 'Competition as a cultural phenomenon'. It was a dazzling performance, a pyrotechnic display of stimulating insights, the intellectual content of which was perhaps accentuated by comparison with the preceding paper, which dealt with the problem of competition in a more aridly formal way. The speakers in the discussion – including Werner Sombart, the economists Emil Lederer and Adolf Löwe and myself – applauded Mannheim. There was only one clearly hostile voice, that of Alfred Weber. And I shall now say something about the antagonism between these two men, which, as far as I know, showed itself publicly, without concealment, for the first time on that occasion. It was not uncharacteristic of the situation of German sociology and *cum grano salis* of German society in the 1920s. For me it was a continuation and a new version of the conflict I had first come across in Thomas Mann's *Betrachtungen eines Unpolitischen*, in the dispute between the conservative Thomas and his more left-orientated brother Heinrich Mann and those like him. I knew both Weber and Mannheim; the flaring of hostility between them brought home particularly vividly to me, a newcomer, how strong were these political differences or, to put it differently, how much Mannheim's and Weber's own sociological opinions were determined by that competition between the parties, the imprint of which on the 'spiritual' (*geistig*) sphere, as it was still called, was the subject of Mannheim's lecture.

I need not go into Mannheim's talk in detail as it is reprinted in the selection from his work edited by Kurt H. Wolff.[7] But perhaps I might highlight some aspects which clarify the nature of this controversy between two leading sociologists of the time.

Mannheim was without doubt the challenger. I have often wondered – but never been able to decide – how far he was aware of it himself. I myself, as the younger and far less powerful man, was never a danger to him. Our collaboration in Heidelberg, and later in Frankfurt, was virtually without friction. But with older people, especially if they claimed higher status, he quickly got into a competitive struggle that he waged quite harshly and implacably. When he had to go into exile and was offered a post at the London School of Economics, he soon enough got entangled in rivalry with the resident sociologist, Morris Ginsberg, who had helped him get the post. I am fairly sure that he was hardly aware of this compulsion in his life. As I have mentioned, Mannheim possessed an almost childish, and at any rate disarming, innocence. Morris Ginsberg, a pupil of Hobhouse, was a shrewd critic of all slovenliness in sociological thinking. He had a strong moral sense and was interested in philosophical and sociological problems of ethics. For Mannheim it was beyond doubt that he himself was the better sociologist. Perhaps he was. But he didn't hesitate to say so. His lectures were lively and interesting. The students flocked to him.

Morris Ginsberg, a slightly negativistic but goodhearted man who in his own way was no less intelligent than Mannheim, was mortally wounded. The situation finally became intolerable. Ginsberg declared: him or me. And his college, the LSE, as was inevitable, stood by their own man and let the newcomer go.

But at the time of the Zurich sociologists' congress that lay far off in the unknown future. Later, in the first year of the war, in Cambridge – where the LSE had been evacuated – when Ginsberg, still with bitterness in his heart, told me about this painful trial of strength with Mannheim, I remembered Alfred Weber's agitated speech at that sociologists' convention in 1928.

Mannheim began with an introduction setting out his own theoretical position in general terms, which for anyone with ears to hear was also his political position. With regard to the importance of competition for intellectual products, he said, there are two extreme positions. The first ascribes to competition at best a peripheral role in the genesis of intellectual products; the second ascribes to it an absolutely constitutive role. In the latter case, therefore, intellectual products are subsumed under social life. In contradistinction to both these extreme views, he himself, said Mannheim, attached only a contributory role to competition. As can readily be seen, these were code-words. They defined Mannheim's standpoint as non-idealist and not absolutely materialist, though partly acknowledging that social determinants such as the competition of political parties co-determined the form of intellectual products.

Anyone who reads Mannheim's lecture today will easily understand why his arguments, conducted at an intellectual level seldom encountered and with their wealth of new ideas, had an extremely fascinating impact on many listeners. One could feel how the subject of 'The importance of competition in the intellectual sphere' suited Mannheim down to the ground. He had given it a completely impersonal and objective form, and probably had no idea that it also had a very personal signi-ficance, and that he was talking at the same time about a central theme of his own life. At any rate, in this talk he created a framework of new ideas that bore witness to his genuine sociological intuition. There were (and are) as yet no complementary empirical studies that could have fully demonstrated the fruitfulness of such ideas. It is undoubtedly a pity that systematic studies of ideology have not been among the everyday concerns of sociology up to our time. But perhaps, for that, theoretical and empirical models would be needed for the careful detailed work entailed by such studies, especially a theory that still lies a long way off, namely a theory of human knowledge as a long-term social process.

As his starting point, and by way of contrast, Mannheim chose the competition-free uniformity of the world-view and style of thinking of the medieval church. After the breakdown of this unity a multiplicity of competing social entities established themselves in Europe, comparable to the multitude of seeds released when the seed-case of a plant bursts. Each of these entities, such as the court, nobility, patriciate, middle and lower-middle class, had a world-view and a style of thinking peculiar to itself that could be explained by its existential location, its social situation and interests.

Here and throughout his work Mannheim uses as a technical term the 'being-relatedness' (*Seinsbezogenheit*) of thought and knowledge, in a clear allusion to the Marxian usage where 'being' is opposed to 'consciousness'. Here he took over in its entirety the Marxian dualism which makes thought and knowledge appear as something existing outside social being, thus bringing being and consciousness into a causal relationship to each other – with being as the cause and consciousness as the consequence.

The relativization and destruction of all thought and knowledge by subsuming it, as an effect, under a thought-less material being stands and falls with the assumption of this existential dualism. In this regard, Mannheim went to the bitter end. He was prepared to relativize everything, including his own position. Now and then he pointed to Descartes as a model. Everything should be doubted. That was the ideal. But in the case of Descartes his own thought remained beyond doubt and destruction, remaining the fixed pole in the flux of phenomena. In

Mannheim's case it was never quite certain whether any secure reality-congruent knowledge – which is after all available in abundance – actually survived intact.

He went further, describing how, from the multitude of social entities and forms of thought released by the disintegration of the medieval unity, a number of competing, being-related thought platforms emerged; it happened by a kind of concentration process that he compared to the economic concentration of many markets into larger markets. Through the effect of competition, the concentration of various national enlightenment movements into the platform of liberalism provoked the formation of a conservative platform. He described the special nature of the liberal and conservative platforms in some detail, relativized both by pointing out briefly the social standpoints connected to them and, in so doing, mentioned in passing the name of Alfred Weber. With Mannheim one was never sure whether he was aware of the relativizing and destructive character of his remarks on liberalism. But there was no doubt that Alfred Weber saw them as destroying his philosophical and political creed, and perhaps even as relativizing the social and political creed of his revered brother Max. Intentionally or not, it was recognizable to everyone as a challenge to Alfred Weber; and on him it worked like a red rag to a bull.

Mannheim continued calmly on his way. He tried to make clear the 'being-relatedness' of the various political platforms and their polarization by their different standpoints towards one and the same problem. To do so, and perhaps in all innocence, he chose a problem from among Max Weber's concerns, the problem of value freedom. Without doubt, Alfred Weber saw his own social creed, like that of his brother Max, as a variety of liberalism, and it cannot be denied that Mannheim's account of liberalism did not really fit Alfred Weber's creed, although Mannheim referred quite directly to Alfred Weber and a quotation allegedly from him. Alfred Weber may have taken this account of him as a caricature.

Liberalism, Mannheim went on, had a strongly rationalist temper. Its exponents sought to distinguish neatly between the

rational and the irrational and to liberate the former from the
latter, and therefore from valuations. While Mannheim himself
sought to demonstrate the total permeation of all thought,
proletarian as well as bourgeois, by the being-relatedness of
interests, he here presented the world-view of Max and Alfred
Weber as the polar opposite to his own. The liberal bourgeoisie, he said, wanted in a typically intellectualist manner to
do away with the irrationality of the tensions between those
who thought differently from each other, and replace it by the
uniformity of *ratio*, of human reason. Moreover, liberals and
democrats, as parties of the centre, had a tendency, in keeping
with their social position, to seek a mediating basis for discussion. Understanding of the antithetical character of valuations
and ideas rooted in antithetical being-situations was lacking,
he argued, in liberals and democrats.

In a similar way, Mannheim administered his medicine to
conservatism and socialism. On the latter, on the outlook of a
proletariat awakening to its class consciousness, he said that
the irrationally of its world view could be discerned not only
in the concept of valuation but in that of interest. Here he distinguished between two tendencies. One, related to liberalism,
was no more aware than that ideology, according to Mannheim,
of the being-dependent, and therefore ideological, nature of all
thought. The other, the line of Marx and Lukács, was aware
of the interest-dependent nature of all thought but neglected
to apply this insight to itself. This tendency, although its thought
was no less interest dependent than that of any other social
creed, simply postulated a preestablished harmony between its
own thought and truth. The class interests of the proletariat
are here quite simply equated with the interests of the whole
of humanity, so that the class consciousness of the proletariat
appeared as the adequate and correct consciousness of reality.

As can be seen, Mannheim was very thoroughgoing in his
total relativization of all partisan systems of belief. It may be
noted that the coded language of the sociologists of the 1920s
was somewhat unlike that of the sociologists of the 1980s.
And the difficulties that arise because the fashionable keywords

of one generation are not properly understood by the next can remind us that the longevity of research recorded in books or articles is greater the simpler the exposition and the less use is made of fashionable, generation-dependent code-words. I have attempted to present the total relativization and ideologization of the whole spectrum of the thought and beliefs of our day, which, despite all the qualifying clauses, formed the centrepiece of Mannheim's sociology, by means of one representative example. Mannheim's skill at showing all political beliefs and forms of thinking as ideology seems to me thoroughly fertile. But I am also sure that we do not need to stop short at this relativization.

In this context, however, I should like to confine myself to evoking the memory of the controversy between Alfred Weber and Karl Mannheim that suddenly burst from behind the scenes to centre-stage at that gathering of sociologists. Reading the record of the proceedings of the Sixth German Congress of Sociologists today,[8] it is easy to overlook the fact that Alfred Weber's contribution to the discussion that followed Mannheim's lecture marked the sudden emergence into broad daylight of a conflict between the two Heidelberg sociologists which had long been in existence but had usually been veiled in polite formalities – a conflict which also throws some light on the situation of sociology in the 1920s. Intentionally or not, Mannheim had certainly provoked Alfred Weber's ire to some small extent by his relativizing account of liberalism and his half-concealed attack on Max Weber's idea of a possible liberation of sociological studies from political valuations. He can hardly have failed to notice that in Alfred Weber's circles he had himself quite often been characterized as an intellectualist, if not exactly a *Zivilisationsliterat*. To have now turned the tables and, hiding behind the code-word of liberalism, to have denounced Alfred Weber in his turn as an intellectualist, was the supreme irony.

Alfred Weber was a polite and civilized man but, as I have said, also a passionate one. In this case he had difficulty in hiding his anger. He would dispense, he said, with the customary polite preamble, the *captatio benevolentiae*, although, he added courteously, the admirable lecture undoubtedly merited it. He also agreed with some of Mannheim's remarks on what he called being-dependence. But – and now he addressed himself directly to Mannheim:

the real issue is what lies behind your way of seeing things, and I do not think one can do justice to your ideas without trying – at the risk of being mistaken – to take a brief look behind the scenes... What, then, is the real, vital significance of the relativization of thought – as you called it – that you have made so brilliantly probable to us today?

When it came to improvising in open discussion, Alfred Weber was not a particularly good speaker, especially when he was agitated. Like many easily excited but self-controlled people he found it difficult to make a direct, open attack on someone else without circumlocutions, and indeed apologies. On this occasion he needed more than twenty minutes – more than the time allowed to speakers – to express his irritation directly. But although he sometimes stammered slightly under the pressure of his emotion, and did not finish his sentences, his arguments themselves were perfectly clear. Of course there was being-dependent thought, he said, but there were also other kinds. And not all being-dependent thought was of the kind that Mannheim had described. Scientific thought was clearly not being-dependent and relativizable in Mannheim's sense. And one had to regard it as an open question whether the mythic thinking of the Greeks and other peoples did not bring to light aspects of the human condition that could not be relativized in the manner described. Moreover, Weber went on, the being-dependence of thought was more diverse than Mannheim had indicated. Every historian knew that the modes of thought of the Greeks and other ancient peoples, and quite generally the categorial apparatus of simpler peoples, differed from our own. That was another kind of being-dependence of thought that deserved investigation, and the same was true of the differences between national modes of thinking. The French had concepts that could hardly be translated into German, and vice versa.

And then he brought himself to say what for him was decisive. It also contained the answer to Mannheim's stigmatizing of liberalism as intellectualist:

> What I find wanting in your arguments is a recognition of intellectual creativity as the basis of action, even the action of classes, for example. What I reject is the reduction of all these things ultimately to intellectual categories supplemented by a few sociological ones which – pardon me – belong to the old materialist view of history. You have spoken about social power positions, of aspirations arising from them, of a public interpretation of existence that is combined with these power positions and aspirations ... What is that but a materialist conception of history reiterated with extraordinary subtlety and brilliance? In essence it is nothing else... I only want to go on record: it is my opinion that this sublimated intellectualism, as I would call it, that, with extraordinary grace and delicacy, subsumes problems which are ultimately of a spiritual nature under these categories without defining their limits, must naturally have exactly the same effect... as the crude intellectualism represented by the old materialist view of history.

I myself then tried – in the limited time available to a young sociologist as yet without office or status – to interpret the antithesis between Weber and Mannheim (not quite correctly) in terms more familiar to me today as the disagreement between an exponent of thinking in eternal laws and an exponent of thinking in structured processes – not quite correctly, since Mannheim, while aware of the flow of history, saw it relativistically as a mere unstructured coming and going. He could not go beyond relativism because the nature of long-term, unplanned but directional social processes – including that of knowledge – still lay beyond his horizon.

What this debate illuminates particularly clearly, it seems to me, is the central role played in German sociology of the 1920s by the argument over the work of Marx and the materialist conception of history. Mannheim's sociology, like that of Max and Alfred Weber, can really only be understood as different forms of this protracted debate with Marx's doctrine of history. They were all attempts to go beyond the Marxian theory of society and history. One way in which Mannheim did this was by trying to apply the dualistic idea that being determines consciousness to Marxism itself. Max Weber did it more circumspectly – for example, by trying to use the concept of the economic ethos of religions to bolster the hypothesis that religions can play an active part in the shaping of economic structures precisely through their economic ethos. Alfred Weber tried to go beyond Marxism by attributing a relative autonomy to culture in relation to economic developments, and also by contrasting the sphere of the empirically identifiable interests of social groups with an intellectual and spiritual sphere that could hardly be grasped by empirical means.

Perhaps I ought just to add that this debate and the problem of how sociology is to develop beyond the Marxian theory is no less acutely topical now than it was in the 1920s. But it seems to me that all attempts to circumvent this obstacle standing in the way of the further development of sociology are in vain. Marx created a theory of long-term social processes attributing the function of the motor of the whole of social development to a partial sphere of this development. I am sure that this hypothesis cannot be bypassed. It is indispensable. Every future sociological theory will, it seems to me, contain at its core a theory of long-term social processes.

What can also be said with confidence today is that a restricting of the motive force of social processes to a single sphere of communal life, the economic sphere, cannot do justice to the demonstrable facts. Forces other than economic ones are also at work in the unplanned development of society. They include, in particular, the forces acting on social development through conflicts between states or, at an earlier stage, between tribes – that is, through the competition of large and small survival units. They also include forces acting on social development through progress in the evolution of means of orientation, that is, knowledge. Indeed, the need for orientation, for knowledge, is no less fundamental than the need for bread, for something that can satisfy hunger, nor can the one be satisfied without the other. The need for knowledge – including the knowledge of how to satisfy hunger – cannot be met without satisfying hunger, which in its turn cannot be satisfied without knowledge. One of the most important tasks facing us is to liberate human knowledge from the anathema laid on it by sociological relativists and economic materialists on the one hand and philosophical nominalists on the other. The development of the means of production, of the means of violence, of self-control and of the means of orientation are intertwined, interdependent, and at the same time they have a relative autonomy. None of the four can be reduced simply to a superstructure of one of the others. There is a limited number of forces of a different kind, but these four already give us an idea of the direction in which to proceed.

The smouldering conflict between Alfred Weber and Karl Mannheim, which flared briefly into public view at that Zurich sociologists' convention, reminds me of a problem I myself encounter constantly. Scholars can wound each other very deeply, they can use well-founded and well-aimed attacks to devalue the life's work of another. When, and to what extent, is it necessary and justifiable to do so? For many years I refrained from criticizing the books of living authors, but then I felt that this could not always be avoided, and since then I have realized that the open attack and the struggle of minds is sometimes inescapable. It is a difficult problem. One threatens the life's work of other people. Certainly, if possible, one should wait until they are dead.

Notes on the Jews as part of an
established–outsider relationship

What I have to say here about the Jews is really part of my
account of my apprenticeship, of what learning taught me. It is
a singular experience to belong to a stigmatized minority while
at the same time being wholly embedded in the cultural flow
and the political and social fate of the stigmatizing majority. I
cannot say that the problems of identity arising from belonging
simultaneously to a German and a Jewish tradition have ever
worried me unduly. I have never made a secret of the fact that
I am a German Jew by origin. I expect people can see it. At
the same time, from early on, while I was at school, I felt a deep
sympathy for the French language and cultural tradition. Fate
has seen to it that, quite late in life, I have formed just as great
a sympathy for the language and cultural tradition of England.
The long years I spent in England from 1935 have been an
extraordinary enrichment to me, a 'blessing in disguise' – a terrible disguise, to be sure, the Jewish fate of being repeatedly
exiled, but a blessing nevertheless.

Precisely because of this fate, I cannot overlook, even in these
fragmentary notes, what I learned from the course of Jewish
destiny. But to talk about it I shall have to broaden the discussion. Otherwise my sociological conscience will leave me
no peace.

It is easy to misunderstand the problems of the Jews in
the German society in which I grew up because it is not
clear what kind of problems these are. People talk of a racial
problem, or perhaps of an ethnic or a religious problem. But
however much a specific religious or cultural tradition may have
influenced the social position of the Jews in Germany, the
decisive factors for the problems arising from the existence of
a distinguishable minority in Germany were really of a social,
and therefore sociological, kind. The underdevelopment of
sociology as a branch of knowledge means that the structure
of the human problems at issue here has not been clarified

as a sociological problems which can then be addressed and solved.

It is not unlikely that the experiences I myself had from an early age as a Jew in Germany contributed to the attraction that sociology later exerted on me. I have never been under any illusions about that. Culturally attached very strongly to the German tradition, I belonged through my personality structure to a despised minority group. Although I had detached myself from this group's most obvious distinguishing feature, its special religion, the particular fate of the minority – a minority that, moreover, had been persecuted and oppressed for centuries – that is, the social fate of the group, found unmistakable expression in my personal habitus, and in my self-consciousness and my thought.

Later, I incorporated many of these experiences in a sociological theory, the theory of established–outsider relationships.[9] Jews, like many other outsider groups in imperial Germany, were denied access to a whole range of social opportunities. There are many parallels, in other countries too, to this closing of ranks by the established against outsiders, and to the exclusion of the latter from many established positions and from the power opportunities they provide. An obvious example are the black and Hispanic groups in the United States. The American Ku Klux Klan demonstrates the deep resentment that can arise in members of a majority, especially those who feel threatened in their own status, injured and insecure in their feelings of self-worth. They are particularly threatened when a socially inferior, despised and stigmatized outsider group is in the process of demanding not only legal but social equality, when its members begin to take up positions in the majority society that were previously closed to them, and thus come into direct competition with members of the majority, and when they perhaps even move into positions which give the despised people higher status and greater power opportunities than those of the insecure lower-status groups of the established.

A despised and stigmatized, relatively powerless outsider group is tolerated as long as its members are content with the inferior position that the established consider appropriate to this group, and as long as they behave like subordinate, submissive people as befits their low status. As long as the black people remain slaves and the Jews small traders or pedlars wandering the country as recognizable ghetto members in alien dress the tension between established and outsiders, though of course always present, is at a relatively low level. It rises when members of the outsider group rise in society or when the outsider group strives for legal and social equality with the superior established groups. In these cases very difficult problems of identity usually arise for both groups. I cannot go into them here. It is enough to say that in this case, for the established groups, the order of things that seems natural to them begins to totter. Their superior status, which forms an integral element of the individual feelings of self-worth and personal pride of many of their members, is threatened by the demands of a despised outsider group not only for social equality but for equal human value. The competition for social opportunities with members of their own group is taken for granted. But to have to compete with members of a despised outsider group seems humiliating and intolerable, especially in the transitional period when everyone is aware that these opportunities were previously a monopoly of the established and were closed to people of the outsider group.

The Jews were for many centuries a despised and stigmatized outsider group in Christian societies. As a result of this long history, the very word Jew carried contemptuous, insulting undertones, not very different from the word 'nigger' in English. As a child, even I hesitated to say the word Jew. One became aware early on that this word was used far and wide as a term of abuse with undertones of the most profound contempt. This was undoubtedly a general, European problem. A whole range of factors contributed to the special difficulties this established–outsider problem brought with it in Germany. Here, I shall mention two of them.

The encompassing German society had itself only recently risen – after 1870 – from an often humiliating, low-status

position among the established European nation states to a
position of relatively great power. Its consciousness of status and
identity was therefore particularly insecure and vulnerable, compared to that of the older, long-unified nations.[10] The Jewish
minority, outsiders in their own country, irritated the Christian
established groups all the more, provoked especial hostility,
because the established groups were themselves still uncertain
about their status and identity as a result of their own historical
situation. There was thus a tendency in Germany to oscillate
from one extreme to the other, from a feeling of humiliation
to one of unique greatness and importance in world history. Of
course, among the various classes in Germany there were distinct
gradations in the hostility towards the Jewish outsider group.
With slight exaggeration, one might say: the more socially insecure, the more anti-Semitic. Thus, in South Africa it is precisely the poorer whites, who are least sure of their own status
and human value in the eyes of others and in their own, who
are usually especially sensitive to any attempt to grant the
oppressed and stigmatized outsiders, the 'Kaffirs' – in this case
the majority – equality and access to all social opportunities.

The second difficulty was connected with the fact that the
Jews were, with very few exceptions, effectively excluded from
many social opportunities and positions in imperial Germany –
or instance, from the higher echelons of bourgeois and noble
society, from the colour-bearing student fraternities, from careers
as officers, diplomats, higher civil servants, university professors, etc. Nevertheless, in the fields which were open to them,
especially commerce and culture, they did not behave at all in
a manner befitting the lowly status conferred on them as a
despised minority group. They took their legal equality seriously
and behaved as if they were Germans. Outsider groups in a
similar position within European nation-states, for instance,
the gypsies, usually remained clearly inferior, culturally and
economically, to the established groups. With the German Jews
at the beginning of this century that was no longer the case.
Apart from the Jewish immigrants newly arrived from the east,
they were culturally assimilated and economically equal. Because

of this – and perhaps also because of their long tradition as a nation of the book, among whom special value was attached to intellectual work – they did not internalize the humiliating and repellent image that the great majority of the established had of them. The regularity that I was later to observe in other established–outsider relationships applied here, too, (and perhaps I perceived it in other cases because I had experienced it, so to speak, in my own flesh and blood). This regularity is as follows: the more powerful of the established read off the we-image of their own group from the minority of the best, and the they-image of the despised outsiders from the minority of the worst.[11]

There are cases when a despised and humiliated outsider group internalizes the devaluing image the more powerful established group has of it. A despised group of people then has a humiliating and soiled image of itself. For the majority of German Jews at the beginning of the twentieth century, and probably for a good many of them even in the nineteenth century, that was not the case. The insults and accusations they were exposed to, and their humiliating existence as outsiders, were sometimes unpleasant and painful, but did not go to the heart of their feeling of self-worth. They were *de facto* people of the second rank, but they did not therefore see themselves as second-class people. I wish there were more studies of the we- and they-images of groups which find themselves in a changing established–outsider relationship to each other. What it means to dark-skinned people to walk around with dark faces in a society dominated by light-skinned people can be seen from the great exertion they have had to make, in connection with a small shift of power in their favour, to tell themselves and others publicly that a black face can be beautiful. And the emphatic and often fanatical way that some Muslim groups advocate Islam in our day can be understood as a reaction – as the result of a shift of power – to a long period of humiliation and a deep feeling of inferiority.

There are countless other examples of such we-image problems arising in the course of shifts in the power balance in the relationship between established and outsider groups. A better theoretical understanding of established–outsider problems would certainly be useful in trying to resolve such problems in social praxis.

When I attempt to reconstruct in memory the way my parents and I came to terms with these outsider problems as Jews in Germany before the First World War, I realize that while we were aware of the discrimination against our group and the stigma we were under, we perceived them only as if through a veil, because of the protection of the legal institutions of the Reich and the thoroughly secure life we led physically, economically and culturally. As a child I knew of the existence of the dislike and hatred directed at members of the group I belonged to, but not of its extent. Nor did my parents and their acquaintances have any real explanation of it. They considered themselves Germans, and no doubt concealed the real situation from themselves slightly. Anti-Semitism seemed the work of mostly uneducated or half-educated people on whom – with a kind of counter-stigmatization – we looked with a certain disdain. I only got a realistic picture of the situation after my schooldays, first as a soldier and then as a student.

The image that comes back to me from my childhood is that of an outsider society which tried to conceal from itself much of its social inequality and ostracization in view of its legal and thus its economic equality. The image of the dirty, cheating Jewish pedlar, mumbling in Yiddish and smelling of garlic, that we met with over and over again in Christian German society was too far removed from what we knew about ourselves to be a serious affront. We lived in a somewhat encapsulated world. Thus it was easy to dismiss the occasional public outburst of hatred against Jews as a misdemeanour of uneducated hooligans.

That, at any rate, was the attitude of my father. He had grown up in a state that he himself viewed as a constitutional state under whose protection he had become a wealthy man, borne up by its economic rise. He was a thoroughly straightforward and honest man, sometimes quick-tempered, but incapable of deception. I cannot imagine that either he or my mother, although they sometimes kept things back from me, ever knowingly told an untruth. I saw them for the last time in 1938, when they visited me in London. I begged them to come to stay with me in England, even if it would cause some financial difficulties. My father did not even consider it, and my mother, as was a matter of course, accepted his decision. I cannot forget the words he used to fend off my allusion to the brutality of the Nazis: 'What can they do to me?' he said, 'I've never done anyone any wrong, I have never broken the law in my life.' He had retired from business in 1910 and then held an honorary position as adviser to the tax authorities, finally receiving a minor decoration. He was a German. He had always obeyed the law. What could a German government have against him? Thus the old people returned in their innocence to Germany.

In cities like Breslau the German Jews formed, sociologically speaking, a second-rank society. But, as I have said, they did not see themselves as second-class people. The fact that many Jews clearly did not accept the inferiority attributed to them and that they behaved, in many cases, as if they were people of equal value, irritated many members of the German majority. It was one of the reasons for the recurrent accusations of 'Jewish impertinence', and certainly hardened the feelings of hostility towards Jews.

There are many established–outsider relationships of this type. To perceive this, to lift the problem to the more sober level of scholarly detachment, seems to me of value in coming to terms with the past. It is useful to see both: the recurrent basic problems of established–outsider relationships of this kind, and the special social circumstances regarding people of Christian and Jewish origin in Germany in the first half of this century. There are majority and minority groups with different origins in many states. As the society approaches the stage of integration of a nation-state the tensions between them normally increase. For example, in this phase of the state-formation process the tensions between majority and minority tribes often increase in young African states; they are increasing in the relationship of the indigenous people to the Chinese minority in contemporary Vietnam, and in that of the Armenians to the majority population of Turkey.

Assimilation or the formation of a separate state are, in the long run, alternative ways of dealing with the problem; expulsion or the annihilation of the minority are other alternatives. Assimilation of the outsider group is always a protracted process, needing a period of at least three generations and often more. How far this solution is possible depends on the willingness of the outsiders to be assimilated, and on the ability of the established to assimilate them. In general, established groups which have behind them an unbroken continuity of social and political development over several centuries and who possess a stable we-consciousness of their own value are both more able and more willing to assimilate outsider groups than nations which have had a much-interrupted development, have a deeply insecure and wounded feeling of self-worth, and which, placing unrealizable status demands on themselves, live in the shadow of a more illustrious past and have to find a new role for themselves in a more modest present.

It is far more hopeful – and it is undoubtedly one of the tasks of sociology – to talk about such problems than to conceal them and leave them smouldering unresolved in the background. But this is not the place to do so in detail. Something important would have been missing from these notes, however, if I had omitted to mention this relationship of the established to the outsiders.

Without doubt, it had a decisive formative influence on me in my childhood and youth. On the one hand, as a young person I found myself immersed through my family background and my schooling in the flow of German and therefore European culture; on the other, I belonged to a special group and thus was sometimes exposed to unforeseen and at first incomprehensible abuse to which there was no reply. I gradually became aware that I belonged to a minority excluded from much that was going on in Germany. I do not think that as a child I understood why that was so and, as I have said, my parents could give me no proper explanation for it. But, of course, that was no bad schooling for a future sociologist. It gave a person a good chance of distancing himself from the dominant society, and a sharp eye for the ideological distortion and concealment of social power relationships.

This opportunity to distance oneself from the dominant, and especially the nationalistic ideologies of the established group, practically always associated even in Wilhelmine Germany and more strongly in the Weimar Republic – as in other countries as well – with belligerent slogans against the Jews, was, of course, only one of the peculiar experiences that came one's way when growing up in a widely stigmatized outsider group. Later one found oneself facing the question: what was it that bound one to the tradition of a group whose most obvious distinguishing feature was the peculiarity of their religion, if one's own beliefs had been completely secularized? Only very gradually, and in conjunction with my sociological insight, did I realize that the social peculiarity brought about by a person's origin, above all the fact of growing up within a stigmatized outsider group, has *per se* a strong, shaping influence on the mentality of the young person concerned. And the special religion, even though increasingly secularized, probably continued to act as a peculiarity of his cultural tradition for some time. It manifested itself, for example, in what I referred to provisionally for my own purposes as the society-specific features of conscience formation. I suspected – and it was really no more than a conjecture – that in the Jewish tradition the sense of the sinfulness of human beings, and thus the tabooing of their animal impulses, especially sexuality, is less oppressive, and that differences of this kind are maintained, given social continuity, despite increasing secularization. The same applies to the taste for emotively charged metaphysical religious assumptions; they remain alien to me. I have sometimes played with the supposition that my own ability, in breaching the dominant taboos, to perceive the changing ways in which civilization deals with elementary impulses may be linked to such a peculiarity of conscience formation.

It is for me a completely open question whether my own strong desire to eliminate unclear or incorrect passages from my own writings as from those of others has a similar origin. Rather it may be a part of a family tradition. Here I feel somewhat the same as my father. After he had retired, the tax authorities kept sending him some of their difficult cases, which, to their mutual embarrassment, sometimes concerned acquaintances of his. They all came along with their advisers and account books, often confidently and nonchalantly, and went home after a few hours, sometimes somewhat depressed. Seemingly without especial difficulty, my father found out whether and where there was something not in order in their books. Sometimes it was just errors, sometimes deliberate deception. My father had a deep aversion to such muddying or falsifying of accounts, as I myself have to mystifying or misleading passages in scholarly books, and I fight as best I can against their appearance in my own. The difficulty is that, especially in the field of social life, the traditional language, the tools of our thought, the concepts themselves, often harbour falsifications and distortions within them. At times this makes the work of sociologists difficult indeed.

Too late or too early – the context of process or figurational sociology

To recall the presociological experiences of a sociologist is not entirely without value in understanding his development. A long life has its advantages, not only for oneself, but for the scholarly work one has to do. One can compare many sets of social circumstances through which one has lived.

In the late twentieth century sociological research and teaching have become professionalized and bureaucratized to a high degree, as happens with established academic disciplines, very often along the lines of models borrowed from the scientific and philosophical establishment. In such a situation it is of some use, it seems to me, to recall the experiences of an earlier time when that was far less the case. At that time, as I have mentioned, people coming from other disciplines were only just beginning to create models for research and teaching in sociology, continuing the work of the great sociological pioneers of the nineteenth century. But the professionalization and bureaucratization of sociology, the practical advantages of which are undisputed – and are indeed unavoidable given the present conditions under which the human sciences operate at universities – have also brought with them a certain narrowing of sociology's perspective, a certain impoverishment of its imagination and sensibility. Thus it would not be without interest to ask what, at that time, induced a large number of people who had originally studied other subjects to turn to sociology. In this context I must content myself with pointing out the problem as such. It has been slightly neglected and deserves special investigation.

It is precisely members of that early, not yet professional generation of sociologists who are mostly canonized today as authorities of sociology. What pushed them towards sociology in many cases was undoubtedly the realization that in the course of increasing urbanization and industrialization on the level of social activity, a profusion of new problems was arising which history, economics and the other social sciences were allowing to lie fallow because they did not fit into their patterns of problem-solving and were not accessible to their traditional methods. At the same time, these discernible social changes confronted scholars alert enough to see them with an innovative task of great magnitude – the task of elaborating a comprehensive theory of human society, or, more exactly, a theory of the development of humanity, which could provide an integrating framework of reference for the various specialist social sciences.

I myself became gradually aware of this task, vaguely in the Heidelberg period and somewhat more sharply while I was in Frankfurt. This task of constructing a central theory of sociology that would be close to empirical facts and thus testable and correctable, the task of laying the foundation of a theoretical structure on which later generations could build, and then either reject, correct or develop further – I pursued this task more and more consciously through all the many special tasks that came to meet me on my winding path. That is not to say that I saw myself in any sense as marking a beginning, an innovator starting from nothing. I was aware that I was wholly embedded in the chain of generations, including that of the sociologists. I was highly conscious of myself as a man of my generations (the plural meaning that my life with the later generations was not without influence on me, even though my life with the earliest and earlier ones penetrated me most deeply). Even the relatively high level of individualization of the sociological imagination was a common trait of many sociologists who came on to the scene before the second great war of the twentieth century. Marx, and to a more limited extent Comte, had already worked on the problem of long-term social processes, although for them the issue was entwined with political ideologies, with social wish-images and ideals of a special kind. Moreover, each of them was still caught up in preoccupations with a particular social process. They had not yet reached the level of reflection from which the question of the how and why of directed long-term social processes could be posed as such.

Nor was broad historical knowledge a rarity among sociologists before the middle of the twentieth century, and many of them were already noting that this knowledge of the past is indispensable for understanding problems of the present. Practically all these people had, like me, acquired their historical knowledge, and thus their knowledge of earlier social structures, not as specialist historians but through their own work, impelled by the sociological problems they were trying to solve. So it was with Marx; as far as his historical knowledge and his other empirical information were concerned, he was largely self-taught. So it was later with Sombart, Max and Alfred Weber and Mannheim, too, as in the latter's preparation for the essay on conservative thinking. They all acquired knowledge of earlier social conditions in the main simply because the questions they were asking, the standpoint from which they made use of 'historical' material, differed fundamentally from the kinds of questions that interested specialist historians.

Later generations who no longer properly understood this difference, whose knowledge and interest were confined narrowly to the present, gave this concern with past social structures, with sociological problems of earlier stages of society, the name 'historical sociology'; but that is a misleading designation. All the sociologists I have mentioned asked sociological, not historical, questions about the past. They often understood something of the dynamics of society. They saw with greater or lesser clarity that the problems and structures of a given human society at the time it existed cannot be explained if they are viewed within a narrow horizon, merely as static data that can be approached in the same way as physical problems and structures – that is, as if they were infinitely repeatable, as if it were a matter of looking for eternally valid laws for them. To view the past, present and sometimes also the future of human societies together, as representing a continuous movement, was therefore nothing uncommon among the generations of sociologists of my youth. They may have had an intuition, even if they did not say it in as many words, that the problems and structures of a given society's present take on a shape very different if they are seen in the light of the past, in conjunction with the long social processes leading up to them, than if they are seen shortsightedly and statically as a mere isolated present.

To arrive on this scene as a latecomer had certain advantages for me, as well as some drawbacks. It was easier for me to recognize how steeped in ideology the existing provisional models of long-term social processes still were. There was a lack of studies that were capable of making social changes over a long time-span sufficiently comprehensible, with the aid of detailed empirical evidence, to allow the existing, often quite speculative models of long-term social processes to be replaced by a different type of theoretical model. By this I mean process models capable of being empirically verified and, if necessary, corrected or refuted. But that was clearly only possible if the investigator was not bound to preconceived, axiomatic beliefs, to one or the other of the opposed ideologies in the party political spectrum of the time.

That was what interested me. I sought to make a contribution to setting this de-ideologization of social theories in motion. It was more difficult than I had thought. In my book *The Civilizing Process* I had, I hoped, succeeded in coming to grips, by means of detailed empirical evidence, with such theoretical problems as that of the civilizing transformation of people and the closely connected change in their level of social integration through the state. I hoped it would be possible for later generations to continue to work on these and other problems of long-term processes, and to correct these first steps if necessary, and thereby at any rate to secure the continuous development of sociology, which in many respects had been lacking up to then.

The theoretical model that came into being in this way also satisfied my desire to demonstrate, not only with general concepts but with the tangible results of research, that it is possible to develop sociological theories that no longer fit into the spectrum of contemporary political parties and social ideals. The emancipation of sociological theories from the hegemony of contemporary political ideologies was, to be sure, no simple undertaking – to start with because this task was not understood. It may take a series of generations before the confusing preponderance of social and political ideologies can be overcome and sociology can safely move forward on the twin tracks of empirical and theoretical research. A single person can only take a few steps along this path; but I hope I have shown that the breakthrough is possible – an escape from the trap set by present-day political beliefs and social doctrines.

The theory of civilization and state formation, the symbol theory of knowledge and the sciences and, more broadly, the theory of processes and figurations that I have tried to elaborate are neither Marxian nor liberal, neither socialist nor conservative. The hidden party doctrines, the veiled social ideals dressed up in scholarly garb seem to me not only fake but sterile. That was – and is – undoubtedly one of the reasons for the difficult reception this theory, and the books in which it is contained, have had. A sociological theory is expected to put forward arguments for or against this or that side in the great conflicts of social beliefs and interests of modern times. It is disorientating to find that that expectation is not fulfilled – although there has certainly been no lack of attempts to interpret my work in that way. For example, it is quite easy to overlook the fact that the concept of the figuration is expressly coined to bypass the ingrained polarization of sociological theories, by which they are divided into those which place the 'individual' above 'society', and those which place 'society' above the 'individual' – a polarization which used to correspond to the main axis of the conflicts of beliefs and interests in the wider world. But as a sociologist one should, of course, resist the pressure coming from these conflicts, especially as in reality that axis has long been overshadowed by others.

I think I can say today that thinking in terms of the figurations that people (including oneself) form with each other has proved its worth in my further work. I do not lack understanding of the fact that the conceptual tool I have tried to elaborate in the form of the concept of figuration has been mainly tested to see what it has in common with earlier theories which placed the collective level of human integration above the individual level, as in Durkheim's and Simmel's proposals, or those of the 'system theorists'. I cannot teach the blind to see, cannot make them understand the difference, however unambiguously I say it. For in the end that depends on a further act of self-detachment, on rising to the next level on the winding stair of self-consciousness, and if people are unable to perform this act of self-detachment, my explanation falls on deaf ears.

The beginnings of such a rise to a higher level were to be found in the preceding sociological theories. Some of the theories of Marx and Weber give evidence of a high degree of detachment, embedded in evidence of their involvement. But they do not yet make detachment and involvement into a sociological problem. They do not take a further step upwards to raise self-detachment as such into consciousness. Until that happens, one cannot help seeing oneself as an individual looking out at society, and thus all other people as 'individuals' outside

and beyond society – or, conversely, society as something existing beyond and outside single individuals.

Until one has taken this further step of self-detachment, and
is able to come to terms with it conceptually, it is, in brief,
difficult to steer the ship of sociology, as of the human sciences
in general, between the ideologies of individualism and collectivism. What distinguishes the concept of figuration from
previous concepts with which it may be compared is precisely
this perspective on human beings that it represents. It helps us
to escape the traditional trap – the trap of polarities like that
of 'individual' and 'society', sociological atomism and sociological collectivism. The very words 'individual' and 'society' often
block perception. If one is able to perform the further act of
self-detachment, one is in a position, in climbing the staircase of
consciousness, to perceive oneself as if on the previous level, as
a human being among others, and society itself as a figuration
made up of many fundamentally interdependent human beings;
only then is one able intellectually to transcend the ideological
polarization of individual and society. The task is as easy as that
posed by Columbus's egg and as difficult as the breakthrough
of Copernicus.

The resistance to this ascent to a higher level of self-consciousness stems in part from a stratum of experience that is
seen most openly in an infant and is never quite submerged: the
stratum on the basis of which one sees oneself as the centre of
the whole world. It manifests itself, for example, in the self-
evident way in which people at earlier stages of development
experienced their land and their group on it as the centre of
the world. It is manifested again, veiled in a thick curtain of
scholarly words, in the solipsistic and nominalist tendencies of
the philosophy of the modern age, from Descartes and Kant to
Husserl and Popper.

Undoubtedly, the resistance to perceiving oneself as a person
forming specific figurations with other people is, by virtue of
this primary egoism in human experience, no less strong than
resistance to the idea that the earth has only a rather incon-
spicuous place in the constellation of planets around the sun,

and that there are a great many stars like the sun. But in addition, the prevalent form of the civilizing moulding of human beings reinforces the illusion that each person is inwardly something that cannot make its way 'outward', and that this 'inner' part is the 'genuine' part of one's person, its 'core' and 'essence'. The theory of the civilizing process makes it possible to perceive that this type of experience of oneself and of individualization is itself something that has evolved, is part of a social process. But against this is pitted the whole weight of the personal feeling of existing inwardly quite for oneself, independently of other people, and the corresponding aversion of people formed like this to the knowledge that even their most personal and essential part is itself something that has evolved in this way in the course of the long development of society.

On the basis of these layers of experience there is a very strong inclination to construe human society from the point of view of oneself, of the 'individual' as an isolated, wholly self-contained being. The resistance to the obvious fact that, from birth, life within figurations of people is one of the basic facts of human existence therefore has its origin partly in a personality structure, a stage in the development of consciousness, which nourishes the illusion that the 'core' of the individual person is, as it were, imprisoned under lock and key in his or her 'inside', and is thus hermetically sealed from the 'outside world', and especially from other people or natural objects.

At the same time, however, a certain political ideology finds expression in this image of humans as *homo clausus*. The notion of the totally independent individual, of the absolutely autonomous but therefore also absolutely free single human being, forms the centrepiece of a bourgeois ideology that has a very definite place in the spectrum of contemporary social and political creeds. Whatever it is called, it is an ideal or a utopia that does not correspond, and cannot correspond, to anything in social reality.

The entrepreneur is often taken as the real social model for this ideal image of the free, self-reliant and independent individual. As the head of a trading, manufacturing or financial organization, independent of bureaucratic state intervention, obeying only his own judgement, as absolute master of his house and in this sense a wholly free individual, in a competitive struggle with other equally free entrepreneurs unhindered by the state, he increases his own wealth and at the same time contributes to the creation of jobs and to the welfare of his country by leading a flourishing enterprise. Now it is quite possible that at the present stage of social development and of the development of individual personality structures, the level of performance, the exertion and inventiveness needed to secure the continued growth of a society's gross national product can only be expected of people through appealing to the egoism of the leading men, by driving them on with carrot and stick – the carrot of profit and the stick of the competition mechanism. Given present personality structures, it is quite possible that such a social arrangement will prove more advantageous from a purely economic point of view – if the goal is continuous growth of the GNP – in competition with an economy wholly planned by the government, administered bureaucratically and which depends solely on commands and obedience without strong personal motivation. But the notion that the owner or, depending on the stage of development in the twentieth century, the director of an economic concern could serve as the pattern for the ideal image of the free individual taking decisions independently of all other human beings can only be understood – sympathetically – as a delusion of the classes concerned, and less sympathetically as a political ideology.

In the late twentieth century the ideological character of this image of the entrepreneur as a model of the free, independent individual has become more pronounced as the monopoly mechanism, whose operation I have examined and described elsewhere,[12] has led in the course of the nineteenth and twentieth centuries to the formation of larger and larger economic units. In place of a relatively large number of relatively small firms, many of which were in fact managed by their owners and their families, so that competitive struggles were often fought out like duels between individuals, a small number of large firms has emerged in many areas of the economy. In accordance with the theory of the monopoly mechanism, smaller economic units can no longer compete in such economic areas. But in the large concerns even the leading men and women are enmeshed in such complex chains of interdependence, and are so dependent in their decision-making on the information and advice of specialized experts, that, applied to them, the ideal image of the free, independent individual seems a caricature rather than a reality. Here 'power' is no doubt being mistaken for 'freedom'.

But the interpretation of free competition as a kind of archetype of the freedom of the individual human being is inappropriate above all because it does not take account of the immanent dynamic and the compulsion exerted by the figuration which freely competing units, whether they are economic enterprises or states, form with each other – the very dynamic I referred to earlier as the monopoly mechanism. The entrepreneur who sees himself as a freely competing individual, because the mechanism of free competition is not strangled or restricted by state intervention, does not include in the scope of his conceptual interpretation of himself the social compulsions to which he himself and his decisions are subject because of the immanent dynamic operating in a field of freely competing units. The answer I was given by an entrepreneur in whose factory I worked for a time, when I asked him why he, a very wealthy man, risked his health in the enormous exertions of his daily work, was very revealing. 'You know', he said, 'it's a hunt. It's a pleasure to snatch the contracts from the competitors, and if you don't do it you soon fall behind.' That was in the 1920s and it was a family firm which, to all appearances, a single man was able to direct with a free hand. But he had enough insight to understand that the representative of a firm which is part of a field of freely competing units cannot decide, for example, whether or not he wants to take part in the competition. He is – by the peculiarity of the competitive figuration – *forced* to compete, if he does not want to lapse into dependence or to go under, that is, go bankrupt. For that is the regularity of every field of freely competing units, which are interdependent precisely as competitors: in a field of freely competing units, within which some units grow larger than the others, a single competitor automatically grows smaller if and because he does not grow larger. As the card player depends on his cards and on the skill of the other players, the entrepreneur is dependent on the market and the skill of his competitors.

Here, at the same time, we have an example of the act of self-detachment that is needed if one is to climb from the stage of consciousness on which one experiences the world from the standpoint of oneself as the centre, to the stage above from which once can see oneself as an individual among others, with whom one forms figurations of a specific kind. From the perspective of the earlier step, one may well regard oneself as the absolutely free master of one's own decisions. From the perspective of the next step up one does not see oneself – as it sometimes appears in keeping with the present political polarities – as a passive object of anonymous social forces existing as it were outside the single human being and driving human beings before them entirely regardless of their actions. One sees oneself rather as someone whose scope for decision is limited because he or she lives together with many other people who also have needs, set themselves goals and take decisions.

Fundamentally, then, it is a simple step that has to be taken in order to orientate oneself better than is now possible in the world that people form with each other. Instead of thinking from the standpoint of the single individual or of social data beyond individuals, it is necessary to think from the standpoint of the multiplicity of people. What we refer to as social constraints are the compulsions that many people impose on each other in accordance with their mutual dependence. But this simple conceptual step seems to be hardly less difficult for many people today than it once was to think of the Earth as merely one solar planet among others. Perhaps the self-detachment involved in seeing one's own person as a person among others is still rather too difficult at present; perhaps it is difficult to entertain the thought that the many individual people never live together in a totally fortuitous and arbitrary manner. The very fact that the others, like oneself, have wills of their own places boundaries on the wilfulness of each of them and gives their communal life a structure and dynamic of its own that cannot be understood or explained if each human being is considered in isolation. They can only be understood and explained if one starts out from the multiplicity of people, from the diverse degrees and kinds of their mutual dependence.

It is, fundamentally, this diversity of human dependences that one refers to in talking of the power relationships of people in a society. To investigate these, it seems to me, is a central task of sociological research. Or, to put it more exactly: it should be a central task. Without defining and explaining the power relationships of groups, macro- and microsociological studies remain incomplete and vague, and ultimately sterile. In an investigation of this kind, special attention needs to be given to changes in power relationships and the explanation of them.

I have attempted to develop a sociological theory of power and at the same time to show – as in my book *The Court Society* – how one can work with such a theory. But it is still hard to gain a hearing for that theory too. There is clearly a special reluctance to perceive changing power balances as an ubiquitous feature of all human relationships – as I showed, for example, in my book *What is Sociology?* A good example of this reluctance is the marginal role played by the concept and problem of power in the theoretical works of Max Weber. In some of his empirical works, and especially his early study of the workers in the region east of the Elbe and in some letters, Max Weber showed an often infallible eye for problems of power. But in his sketch of a grand theory he tried as best he could to suppress the problem of power relationships from his typology of relationships of imperative control. His extraordinary sociological sensibility enabled him to perceive quite clearly that the monopoly of physical force is one of the essential central institutions of a state. Command of such a monopoly, the ability of a given ruler to compel the citizens to follow the social norms and laws by the use of the mere threat of physical compulsion, is undoubtedly one of the decisive sources of power in any form of state rule. But in Weber's theory of imperative control, which certainly refers to control by the state, the problem of power is touched on at best marginally. From time to time he lets drop the remark that control can be 'conferred'. Apart from that, the question that most interests Weber is why individuals submit themselves to being ruled. Their motives for this, such as the affective bond of the ruled to the ruler, are the primordial concern of his typology.

In Weber, as in other cases, the basic liberal attitude that forces him to construe society from the standpoint of the single individual has a disastrous effect on the elaboration of a sociological theory. I am not speaking here of the merit a liberal attitude might have in the party political struggle in our day. I am speaking of the distorting effect a liberal ideology must have on the construction of sociological theories. It constrained Max Weber, as it does other sociologists striving to evolve a sociological theory, to present the relation of individual and society as if the individual human being existed in the first place entirely independently of society, and therefore of other people, and only came into contact with other people in a secondary and, so to speak, retrospective way.

Max Weber's famous example of what is social action and what is not, that is, what is 'purely individual' action, shows up very vividly this egocentric basic attitude, according to which a human being experiences himself or herself primarily as an isolated individual. If a lot of people put up their umbrellas at the same time when it starts raining, that, for Weber, is not a social action. As so often in his sketch of a theory, Weber fails to identify this non-social action positively in conceptual terms. But it is quite clear what he is getting at. Here each individual is acting for himself; the opposite of social action that Weber constructs here represents, in his view, a 'purely individual' action. Weber was not yet in a position to ascend to the level of self-detachment from which he might have perceived the many people opening their umbrellas as it starts to rain as a social figuration, that is, as members of a society in which it is usual to protect oneself from rain with an umbrella. He was

stuck on the level of consciousness where he perceived himself –
and then, on the same pattern, every other person – as a figure
existing primarily on his own. The action of such a person only
becomes social, for Weber, through an act of will by the individual, when such action is orientated towards other people in
the consciousness of the person taking the action. This theoretical notion embodies, as I have said, not only a particular
political ideology, but also the primary experience of a child which
feels itself to be the centre of the world, a monad existing in
isolation.

Into this experiential pattern Weber's basic epistemological attitude, with its neo-Kantian stamp, fitted smoothly and seamlessly.
For the windowless monad, *homo clausus*, the egocentric human
being, also formed the starting point of his theorizing. As the
subject of knowledge the isolated person stands looking out at
the whole world. The images of this world 'inside' the head are
separated from the world out there, the 'outer' world, as if by an
invisible wall. Thus he can never really know whether or how far
these 'inner' images match the 'outer' world. In Kant the idea of
the external world was generally limited to the world of inani-
mate objects. In Weber it referred primarily to human society. As
conceived by Weber this society, in keeping with his atomistic
outlook, was really only a barely ordered hotchpotch of many
isolated actions by many isolated people. But as a sociologist one
could bring order into what was in reality the somewhat chaotic
medley of the social actions of many individuals by an idealizing
abstraction of recurring typical structures, by the formation of
'ideal' types. Kant's philosophical idealism, which derived the
order of nature ultimately from the reason of the human being
investigating nature, thus went very well with Weber's sociological
idealism, which derived the order of society ultimately from the
reason of the human being investigating society. Admittedly
this applies mainly to Weber's most generalized sketch of a
theory. In his studies more closely based on empirical data he
often presented verifiable figurational models – such as the city
or the bureaucracy – in a manner completely in keeping with
the normal scientific quest for utmost congruence with reality.

Weber's approach to sociological theory, at the same time atomistic and idealizing, was no doubt one of the reasons why, despite his sharp eye for power relationships in social praxis, he contributed little theoretically to the problem of power. For power problems are – leaving aside a few borderline cases – problems of relationship and dependence. Whether one studies power relationships in the relation of infant and parents, workers and employers, rulers and ruled or of smaller and larger states, they always involve balances of power, usually unstable, that can change. It is difficult to gain theoretical access to this kind of problem from the atomistic standpoint of an originally relationless individual.

An additional factor, perhaps, is that people in the situation of having greater power are more inclined to lose sight of problems of power differences and to conceal them. The situation of those of lesser power, especially if they are in a position to fight for an improvement of their situation, produces, one may assume, a greater disposition to perceive power differences. It is not surprising that Marx, who himself came from an outsider group and identified to a high degree with the working class and its lesser power, perceived and theoretically elaborated a number of specific power problems from his specific angle of vision. He noted that the monopolization of the means of production represented a source of power for the employers in the relation between workers and employers.

But the gaze of Marx and most of his followers was so fixated on this one form of power and on the power differences arising from this monopolization that they were unable to propose an explicit and more comprehensive theory of power. The calamitous influence of this blinkered vision showed itself quite clearly in the first major attempt to put Marx's theory into practice. Marx himself seems to have had the idea that it was enough to eliminate the economic sources of power inequalities, the monopolization of the means of production outside the state, in order to make social inequalities disappear. The practical application showed the inadequacy of this theory with frightening precision; it showed that the elimination of the private monopoly of the means of production is by no means enough to eliminate the hierarchical inequality of the social structure, or to reduce it to the slightest degree. The attempt to put Marx's social theory into practice revealed, in a short time and far more trenchantly than any book could have done, the one-sidedness of its ideological perspective and thus also its theoretical deficiencies.

Marx's theorizing from the standpoint of the industrial proletariat had in common with the ideological theories formed from the standpoint of the liberal bourgeoisie the fact that they both presented the state as servant of the economy. The power chances available to a state government appear in both cases as something secondary as compared to the economic power chances, and to the 'economic sphere' in general. Marx even played with the idea that the state organization as such had no other function than to serve the capitalist class, for example, in protecting property, and that it would disappear when private property was abolished by a revolution. Like most bourgeois social theorists, he thought he could present as an adequate social theory one which was limited to aspects of the internal conditions within a state society. He did not yet see that to be more realistic, that is, more useful in practice, a theory of society has to take account of all the social structures linked to the relations between states, and to the existence of a multiplicity of state societies, in addition to the structures linked primarily to conditions within a given state society. Consequently, he had no means of perceiving that the two interdependent central monopolies of the state organization, those of physical force and of taxation, can have other functions besides protecting the private property of one class, and can therefore continue to exist as means of extreme power even after the abolition of private property. It is questionable whether Marx's notion of a quasi-autonomous economic sphere is applicable at all to stages of social development when the commercial owners of capital, as a quasi-autonomous group, have a high degree of control over the powers of the state – as in the United States at present – or where, by virtue of their power, they can counterbalance the groups who control the resources of the state.

At all events, the ideological shortsightedness of Marx's theory was shown very quickly in the attempt to realize it. The private ownership of the means of production was abolished, but the state organization did not show the slightest tendency to disappear, even with the passage of time. On the contrary, the range of state functions, and therefore the power of the rulers, was increased by the revolution. In this respect the attempt to put Marx's theory into practice showed with particular vividness the disorientation produced by mingling sociological theory with ideological wish-images and ideals. As the revolutionary programme prescribed, control over the entire capital of the state society, which up to then had been largely dispersed in the hands of a whole class of people, was now drawn together and unified; it was concentrated in the hands of the party leaders and the members of the government. This represented a massive increase in the power of the state rulers, as compared to their widely dispersed subjects. The twin government monopolies of the means of physical violence, represented by its control of the military and the police, and of taxation, which made it possible, among other things, to maintain the state apparatus of violence, were now combined, in the hands of a small group of rulers, with monopolistic control over the whole capital of the state society, that is, a monopoly of the means of production. This was quickly followed by the rulers' control of two further monopolies of central importance to the distribution of power chances in a society: the postrevolutionary government claimed for itself the absolute monopoly of the basic means of orientation, especially that of interpreting all social structures past and present, and the monopoly of the right to organize – no group in the country could be organized without the government's permission.

All these monopolies were, and are, means of power. Their concentration in the hands of a small group of people, who were answerable to no one except their own committee for their decisions, thus signified on another level – not the economic but the state level, not in the relation of workers to employers but in that of ruled to rulers – a steep hierarchy, a permanent institutionalizing of inequalities among the people bonded to each other in this state society.

Hand in hand with this unplanned but theoretically foreseeable hierarchization, which reemerged in a tighter, better organized form with the putting of Marx's theory into practice, went limited new forms of equality. They included a broad increase in the opportunities of young members of the working and peasant classes, and especially of women, to rise in society and to pursue careers. They also included a more planned, more purposive industrialization and modernization of the country and a comprehensive state expansion of welfare institutions for the mass of the population, a parallel development to western welfare states. On the other hand, even in the factories the hierarchization of social positions remained at roughly the same level as in the private companies of the west. The private supervisors of workers and employees were replaced by state and party ones.

Both kinds of society, Communist and capitalist alike, remained in reality highly imperfect. They probably both functioned better than most societies at earlier stages of development. But social inequality and poverty remained very great in both. In both cases reality fell very far short of the idealizing images of the ideologies with which they tried to legitimize themselves in their own eyes and in relation to each other. To simplify, one could say that the USSR was still far from being a land of equals, and the USA far from being a land of the free.

If one tries to imagine a more objective sociological view of the two societies, a view less masked by ideologies – if one keeps in mind how blatantly the imperfections of both societies appear when viewed realistically, and how much these imperfections could be reduced if only a fraction of the military expenditure were used to reduce them – one cannot avoid asking the question how the increasing tension between the two great powers, which now threatens the whole of mankind, is really to be explained. The answer, briefly, is that the established groups of both powers, the groups capable of governing, have manoeuvred themselves into a double-bind figuration. For fear of being overwhelmed by the other side, each of these groups tries to overwhelm the other, or at least to become stronger than it, and thus to attain a position of hegemony. Each finds itself in a dilemma which dictates its moves. For fear of being subjugated, they have to subjugate. For fear of falling behind, they have to outdistance their rival throughout the world. What can be done to loosen the fetters of this compulsion?

In posing this question one first of all sees more clearly the central part their opposed social ideologies, their predominant creeds and ideals, play in the hostility between the two great powers. It is not just a matter of letting two societies develop further and then, after a time, deciding through a committee of referees which model has proved more advantageous for the mass of people making up these societies, that is, which society functions better in this sense. At the present stage of civilization, the two models are not seen, in people's consciousness, just as two different blueprints for societies. They take the form of creeds conferring meaning on life, ideologies with the same emotive value as supernatural religions. As such they are perceived, like the supernatural religions of earlier days and perhaps of our own, as demanding exclusivity. Only our pattern of society – so the social blueprint elevated to a social religion insists – can be correct; yours is objectionable, inferior and harmful.

This deeply embedded hostility between the two social models raised to the status of creeds is certainly no accident, for the two ideologies stem from the conflicts within states between two different social classes in industrial societies. But with the conquest of the state apparatus of a great empire by supporters of a creed conceived and elaborated in the name of the less powerful groups in the class struggle, the function of this creed changed. It was transferred from the intrastate to the interstate level; an ideology of class conflict within states became an ideology of international conflicts between states. As was to be expected, this redirection of an intrastate ideology of class conflict to become a quasi-national ideology of state conflict was not confined to one side. The ideology of the other side, too, was now changed from a predominantly internal affair into a quasi-national creed held by a whole state population or at any rate its leading groups.

The remodelling of ideological weapons of the class war as ideological weapons in the struggle between states played no small part in heightening the tensions and conflicts on the international level. One might wonder if the Russian empire and the United States at the present stage of development would not also have become the two most powerful states on earth, and as such rivals, if the process of industrialization and modernization in Russia had proceeded according to the capitalist model. If one envisages this hypothetical situation, it is easy to see that although in this case the dynamic of the monopoly mechanism would in all probability have brought the two great powers into conflict, one decisive factor would have been different. In a conflict, the leading cadres of the two societies would not necessarily have threatened each other with social and perhaps even physical destruction. No matter how much they might have been driven into collision with each other by the dynamic of the struggle between states for hegemony, as capitalists they would have shared the same ideology, the same social faith. But as a result of the transformation of slogans of internal class struggle into international ideologies, the warlike tension between the two great powers means that the ruling cadres of both powers are threatened with mutual destruction. The Communists threaten, should they win, to introduce a communist regime in America, while the American capitalists threaten, should they win, to set up a capitalist regime in Russia. And as both sides, driven by their ideologies, have an image of their own social and physical destruction before their eyes, they represent a deadly threat to each other.

People now attempt to explain the opposition between the two great powers essentially by the fact that the Americans have a capitalist social constitution and the Russians a Communist one. But the difference of their internal social constitutions can hardly make understandable the extent of their enmity or their threat of mutual destruction. If this difference alone were responsible, one could really say: let the Russians build up their Communist state and the Americans their capitalist state. If they did nothing but that, one could really see no reason why they should disturb each other.

We come somewhat closer to explaining the extent and the implacable nature of the enmity if we also consider that the difference of social structures is linked to a difference of social creeds, to a difference between social ideologies that have something of the fixed character of religions. This ideological antagonism impels both the Russians and the Americans to present their own actually quite imperfect social system as the ideal, the best possible system in the world, and to see it as a kind of national mission to help their social system and their social faith to attain predominance in as many other states as possible. Here the Russians have a certain advantage over the Americans as missionaries propagating the Communist system, in that they possess an authoritative book containing a prophecy promising them that the future belongs to their social system and their faith. Both, their book declares, will inescapably spread to encompass the world. No doubt many people in Russia as in America know that the social reality of their countries has great defects and that a great gulf separates it from the ideal image. But at the same time, partly through education and partly through propaganda and social control, the belief in the incomparable value and finality of the Communist system on the one hand and the capitalist system on the other is deeply anchored in the personality structures of the people concerned, as an integral part of their national identity, for which it would be worthwhile, if necessary, to risk one's life and to die.

Part of the reason why the escalation of the double bind which drives the two great powers against each other is so difficult to control is that the quasi-religious emotional root of the social ideologies stands in the way. Treating the social faith in a more relaxed way is certainly one key to loosening the trap of the double bind. Without ideological disarmament, military disarmament is not enough. If there is no major war, capitalists and Communists will have to live with each other for a long time yet, and change as they do so. For neither capitalism nor Communism is a final state.

I do not believe that sociologists can make their contribution to overcoming the great danger in which we find ourselves as long as they are themselves intellectually and emotionally trapped in the ideological dilemma and thus in the great double bind. If a calm sociological study of ideologies and double-bind traps is to be possible, this itself requires a certain degree of detachment.

Notes

1 *Idee und Individuum. Ein Beitrag zur Philosophie der Geschichte* ('Idea and individual: a contribution to the philosophy of history'), extract from a doctoral dissertation ... submitted by Norbert Elias. Doctorate awarded 30 January 1924. Hochschulverlag Breslau. Cf. notes 3 and 4 below.

2 N. Elias, 'Problems of involvement and detachment', *British Journal of Sociology*, 7 (1956), pp. 226–52. This essay forms the first part of a larger study published as *Involvement and Detachment* (Oxford, 1987).

3 As mentioned, only a short extract was printed in 1924. The work was essentially finished in July 1922, although I then had to change some points as a concession to Hönigwald's transcendentalism, with which I disagreed quite radically by that time.

4 More than fifty-six years later, in July 1980, I came across this work once more. Dr Peter Ludes had discovered that the printed extract is still in the library of Breslau University. At his request the Polish authorities kindly sent him a copy; he in turn was kind enough to send one to me.

I, the old man, confronted the young man I had once been not without a certain shock. On the one hand I recognized myself; I found with some surprise that at twenty-seven I had already been working on problems that concerned me later in writing *The Civilizing Process* (Oxford, 1994; German original, *Über den Prozess der Zivilisation*), and then repeatedly, as in the essay 'Zur

Grundlegung einer Theorie sozialer Prozesse' ('Foundation of a theory of social processes'), *Zeitschrift für Soziologie*, 6 (1977), pp. 127–49, i.e. the structure of unplanned social processes.

As early as my dissertation, therefore, I had been puzzling over what I later called 'a sequential order', the specific order within which a later event arises from a specific sequence of earlier events. At that time I was wondering about questions that are still of the utmost interest to me today, e.g. the question of how a later form of state emerges from an earlier one which in turn emerges from a yet earlier one, and why it is the case; or how a later economic form arises from an earlier one, a later form of knowledge from earlier ones and, more generally, how later forms of human social life emerge from earlier ones. Already present as well was the problem of the relation of physical to social time, which was to play such a central role in *Time: An Essay* (Oxford, 1992).

But at that early stage in my learning process I envisaged the succession of stages in a social development as a sequence of mental structures. I would now see their substrate as made up of five-dimensional people of flesh and blood. My earlier view was probably an outcrop of the process model most familiar to a philosophy student at that time: that of Hegel, whereby the reasoning *C is D* could follow from the proposition *A is B*. I did not yet distinguish clearly between 'process' and 'system', but I already understood that a historical fact is a function of its position within this process, and I was pointing towards a fact that is not stated often enough even today: that in human experience it is not only what has gone before that can be posited as the reason for what comes after, for its consequences; in the experience of those who come later even what comes afterwards, the 'consequences', in part determine the way in which something which happened earlier, the 'reason', is experienced and understood. For example, the so-called 'modern age' did not simply emerge from an earlier period we call the Middle Ages; the way in which we experience the Middle Ages is also influenced by the fact that the modern age has emerged from it, and by the way we understand this modern age. That period only became the 'Middle Ages' when seen from the modern age, and to understand the modern age it is necessary to see the Middle Ages as they were before the modern age existed. Similarly, it is useful to imagine this modern age as seen through the eyes of those for whom it has become a 'Middle Ages', and perhaps not even a very civilized one – a useful exercise for people living today, whether or not that other modern age ever comes about.

Of course, it is none too easy when reading the extract to translate the earlier ideas from the frightening philosophical idiom into plain language. It is also clear in this text how I tried to get round my research supervisor's categorical rejection of one of my central arguments with a compromise formula. In the last paragraph I pointed out that, as I had presented the matter, each single idea emerges as a consequence from reasons, and 'can thus even be subject to the laws of the dialectical process'. But I added that 'the idea of validity as a principle of the dialectical process is not subject to its movement.' In this last sentence I made my bow to the philosophical fetish of the concept of validity, which certainly has its place, like any other concept, in the process of the evolution of human thought and can only be understood in terms of its function within this sequential order. But for philosophers, the secularized heirs of theological ways of thinking, it often acts as a symbol of their own aspirations to float in a dimension of eternity above the ceaseless flow of evolution.

It was certainly not easy to break free from the constraints of this highly ritualized philosophical idiom of thought, with its compulsory reduction of processes to states, and its tightly knit system of argumentation. Reading this extract from my dissertation, I saw myself as the horseman riding across Lake Constance. Without fully realizing the danger I was in, I had escaped.

5 Cf. Elias, *The Civilizing Process*, pp. 1–41.
6 Karl Mannheim, 'Conservative thought', in *Essays on Sociology and Social Psychology* (London, 1953), pp. 74–164.
7 Karl Mannheim, *Essays on the Sociology of Knowledge* (London, 1952), pp. 191–229.
8 *Verhandlungen des Sechsten Deutschen Soziologentages vom 17. bis 19. September 1928 in Zürich* (Tübingen, 1929) – discussion of Von Wiese's and Mannheim's lectures, pp. 84–124.
9 N. Elias and J. L. Scotson, *The Established and the Outsiders*, (1965), with a new introductory essay (London, 1994).
10 See N. Elias, *The Germans: Studies of Power Struggles and the Formation of Habitus* (Cambridge, forthcoming).

11 Elias and Scotson, *The Established and the Outsiders* (London, 1965), p. 53.
12 Cf. Elias, 'State formation and civilization', in *The Civilizing Process*, pp. 257–543.

Chronology

———◆◆———

1897	Born 22 June in Breslau, son of Hermann and Sophie Elias
1915	Military call-up, service on the Western Front
1918	Begins studying medicine and philosophy in Breslau, with semesters in Heidelberg and Freiberg
1924	Doctorate of Philosophy
1925	Moves to Heidelberg to start an academic career; meets Karl Mannheim and switches to sociology
1930	Moves to Frankfurt as assistant to Mannheim
1933	Flees from Germany; attempts to find university posts in Switzerland and Paris
1935	Travels to England via Germany; starts to work on *The Civilizing Process*
1940	Hermann Elias dies in Breslau
1941?	Sophie Elias dies in Auschwitz
1935–75	Lives mainly in England; after the war, works in connection with adult education
1954	Lecturer in Sociology at the University of Leicester
1956	Meets Johan Goudsblom at the Third International Sociology Congress in Amsterdam
1962–4	Professorship at the University of Ghana
1965 on	Invitation lectures in Holland (Amsterdam, The Hague) and Germany (Münster, Konstanz, Aachen, Frankfurt, Bochum, Bielefeld). Apartments in Amsterdam (from 1975) and Bielefeld (from 1978)

1977   Receives the Adorno Prize of the city of Frankfurt for the
          whole body of his work
1979–84   Researching and teaching at the Centre for Interdisciplinary
          Research, University of Bielefeld
1984   Settles finally in Amsterdam
1987   Awarded honorary doctorate by the University of Strasbourg
          III
1988   Presented with the Premio Europeo Amalfi for *The Society
          of Individuals* as the best sociology book published in
          Europe in 1987
1990   Dies 1 August in Amsterdam

Select Bibliography

Books by Norbert Elias

The Civilizing Process (1939), trans. Edmund Jephcott, Oxford, 1994 (one-vol. edn).

With J. L. Scotson, *The Established and the Outsiders; A Sociological Enquiry into Community Problems* (1965), with a new introductory essay, London, 1994.

What is Sociology?, London, 1978.

The Court Society, trans. Edmund Jephcott, Oxford, 1983.

Involvement and Detachment (1986), Oxford, 1987.

The Loneliness of the Dying, Oxford, 1986.

With Eric Dunning, *Quest for Excitement: Sport and Leisure in the Civilizing Process*, Oxford, 1986

The Society of Individuals (1987), ed. Michael Schröter, trans. Edmund Jephcott, Oxford, 1991.

The Symbol Theory, London, 1991.

Time: An Essay, trans. Edmund Jephcott, Oxford, 1992.

Mozart: Portrait of a Genius, ed. Michael Schröter, trans. Edmund Jephcott, Cambridge, 1993.

On Norbert Elias

Stephen Mennell, *Norbert Elias: An Introduction*, Oxford, 1992.

Index

absolutism in Germany, 59–61
academic career
  in Heidelberg, 33–42, 83,
    93–105, 109–10
  in Frankfurt, 42–9, 96, 131
  in London, 53–65
  in Leicester, 65–7, 73
  in Ghana, 67–73
  since 1965, 1–2, 67, 74
  honours, 73
Adorno Prize, 73
ambition, Elias's, 22, 36–7,
  38
Amsterdam, Elias in, 2, 74
anti-Semitism
  and established–outsider
    relationships, 19, 121–30
  'Final Solution', 52
  personal experiences of, 12,
    23, 47, 78–9
  threat not perceived, 12–14,
    51–3, 126–7
  in Wilhelmine Germany,
    11–14, 17–18
  see also Jewishness; Jews

architecture and sociology, 41,
  97–8
art
  African, 3, 68, 69, 72–3
  and start of scientific thinking,
    41

Bar-Mitzvah, 85
Bedford College, visiting lecturer
  at, 81
'being-dependence' theory of
  Mannhein, 105–8, 109,
  113–16, 117–18
Bergsträsser, Arnold
  (Heidelberg), 95
Bielefeld
  honorary doctorate, 73
  Zentrum für interdisziplinäre
    Forschung (ZiF), 1–2, 74
Bion, W. R. (Tavistock Clinic),
  63
Breslau
  childhood in, 3–13, 83–5
  return after military service in
    France, 3, 27

Breslau (*cont.*)
  medicine and philosophy
    studies, 27, 29–31, 83, 86,
    88–92
  work in iron foundry, 31–3
  post-doctorate departure from,
    33–4
British Museum, 52–5
Bulgaria, 20

Cambridge, evacuation to, 62,
    112
capitalism, 32, 147–51
'chain of generations', 38, 101,
    132
childhood, 3–13, 83–5
civilization *see* culture–
    civilization antithesis
The Civilizing Process, 52–6,
    61, 134
class structure in Germany,
    France and England, 57–9,
    60
collectivism, 135–7
Communism
  in Germany between the wars,
    41, 43, 95
  ideological nature of, 39, 47,
    144–7, 148–51
competition, social
  and the entrepreneur, 138–40
  and established–outsider
    relationships, 122–3
  Mannheim lecture on, 105,
    110–16
Comte, Auguste, 102, 132
The Court Society, 55, 141
culture, early love of German,
    18–19, 74–5, 84–5, 122
culture–civilization antithesis,

  56–7, 102–4
Curtius, Ernst Robert
    (Heidelberg), 96

death
  attitude to, 15, 80
  German songs about, 24–5
democracy, 45–6
Descartes, René 113–14, 136
disarmament, ideological, 150–1
dissension
  with colleagues, 66–7
  with teachers, 32, 34, 91–2
'double bind', theory of, 22,
    148–51
Durkheim, Émile, 135
Dürrsamen, Fraulein (landlady),
    34–5

Ebert, Friedrich, 28, 61
education
  governesses, 3, 8–9
  Johannes-Gymnasium in
    Breslau, 3, 83–4
  medical and philosophy
    studies, 27, 29–31, 83,
    86–90
  in sociology, 34, 35–6, 83,
    96
Eichendorff, Joseph von, 85,
    103
Elias, Hermann (father)
  character, 3, 6, 7–8, 126–7,
    130
  death, 53
  fears for safety of, 52, 55
  inter-war visits with his son,
    49, 51, 52, 127
  and printing of *The Civilizing
    Process*, 61

see also family
Elias, Norbert (1897–1990)
  childhood in Breslau, 3–13,
    83–5
  military service, 15–27, 86
  medicine and philosophy
    student, in Breslau, 27,
    29–31, 83, 86, 88–92
  philosophy student in Freiberg
    and Heidelberg, 29, 30, 34,
    93
  in Breslau iron foundry, 31–3
  in Paris toy factory, 49–51
  academic career *see* academic
    career
  publications *see* publications
Elias, Sophie (mother)
  childhood memories of, 3,
    6–7, 8
  fears for safety of, 52, 55
  inter-war visits with her son,
    49, 51, 52, 127
  internment and death in
    Auschwitz, 53, 78–9
  see also family
England, attitude to and
    experience of, 19, 51,
    53–67, 121
entrepreneur as social model,
    137–40
established–outsider
    relationships, 121–30

family life, 4, 8–10, 13,
    14–15, 78
  see also Elias, Hermann;
    Elias, Sophie
figurational sociology, 130–51
Florence, and growth of
    science, 41, 98

Foulkes (formerly Fuchs), S. H.
    (Group Analytic Society),
    63–4
France
  attitude to and perception
    of, 19, 50, 56–9, 60, 121
  life in Paris, 49–51
  military experience in, 24, 25
Frankfurt, academic career in,
    42–9, 96
Freiberg, student in, 29, 30
Freud, Anna, 63
Freud, Sigmund, 48, 58, 70–1,
    76
Freudenthal, Grete (friend), 49
Freyer, Hans (sociologist), 98
Frijda, Professor (Paris), 50

Germany
  before World War One, 5,
    10–14, 16–19
  between the wars, 27–9, 36,
    41–9, 51–2, 59–60
  and culture–civilization
    antithesis, 56–7, 103
  early love of German culture,
    18–19, 74–5, 84–5, 122
  feelings about being German,
    10–11, 16–21, 79–80,
    121
  post-World War Two, 73,
    74–5, 78–9
Ghana, career in, 67–73
Gide, André 50
Ginsberg, Morris, 62, 111–12
Glucksmans (Cambridge), 62
Goethe, Johann Wolfgang
    von, 18, 58, 85
Goldstein, K. (Frankfurt), 42
Group Analytic Society, 63

Habilitation, 92, 95, 96–7, 98, 99
health
  in childhood, 3, 14, 15
  effect of military service, 23
  in old age, 2
Heidelberg, 33–42, 93–110
  philosophy student in, 29, 30, 34, 93, 95
  post-graduate career in, 33–42, 93–105, 109–10
Heine, Heinrich, 85
Hiller, Kurt (left-wing intellectual), 103
Hindenberg, General von, 21
Hitler, Adolf, 21, 46–7, 51–2, 60–1
Holland
  grant from Dutch foundation, 50
  recognition in, 73
Hönigswald, Richard (philosophy teacher), 30, 88–9, 91–2
Horkheimer, Max (Frankfurt), 48–9
Husserl, Edmund, 92, 136

idealism, 143–4
  see also realism
identity
  of established and outsider groups, 123
  national, 57, 123–4, 150–1
ideological disarmament, 150–1
ideology
  leading to international hostility, 148–51
  Mannheim on, 37, 106–8, 109

as mythology, 39–40
  self-detachment from, 133–41, 151
  see also mythology; realism
individualism, 134–7
individuals
  as *homo clausus*, 87–9, 100–1, 137, 143
  independence or inter-dependence of, 47, 100–1, 136, 137–41
  utopian myth of freedom and independence, 137–9
inflation, effect of, 31, 33, 91
iron foundry, employment in, 31–3
Isle of Man, internment in, 62

Jaffé, Frau (Heidelberg), 96
Jaspers, Karl (Heidelberg), 35, 83, 95
Jewishness
  Elias's acceptance of, 10, 79–80, 121
  influence on work, 121–2, 126, 128–30
Jews
  as carriers of German culture, 19
  contempt for anti-Semitism, 11, 126
  feelings of self-worth, 11–13, 124–7
  see also anti-Semitism
Jones, Maxwell (Therapeutic Society), 63
Jüttner (mathematics teacher), 84

Kaiser *see* Wilhelm II, Kaiser

Kallius (anatomy lecturer), 86, 91

Kant, Immanuel, 18, 84, 136, 143
  and concept of *a priori* truth, 91–2

Klein, Melanie (Tavistock Clinic), 63

knowledge, human need for, 120

Konstanz, visiting professorship at, 74

Koyré, Alexandre (Paris), 50

Kruger, Dr (philosophy teacher), 84

Lederer, Emil (economist), 110

Leicester, career in sociology faculty, 65–7, 73

liberalism, 47, 114–15, 116, 118, 142

Loewe, Adolf (economist), 110

London, Elias in, 53–65
  at LSE, 62
  lectures at Bedford College, 81
  visit by parents, 51, 52, 127

London School of Economics, 62, 111–12

Löwen (Frankfurt economist), 42

Löwenthal, Richard (Heidelberg), 39

Ludendorff, Erich von, 21

Lukács, George, 83, 115

Mann, Heinrich, 103, 104, 111

Mann, Klaus (Paris), 50

Mann, Thomas, 103, 104, 111
  as subject of Elias's paper, 83, 95

Mannheim, Dr Karl, 1, 36, 104–8, 109–20, 132
  being-dependence theory, 105–8, 109, 113–16, 117–18
  'Competition as a Cultural Phenomenon' lecture, 105, 110–16
  in England, 63, 105, 111–12
  Ideology and Utopia, 96, 105
  relationship with Elias, 34, 37–8, 42, 83, 96
  rivalry with Alfred Weber, 34, 104, 109–20
  supervision of *Habilitation*, 96

Marx, Karl, 35, 48, 132
  doctrine of society and history, 95, 115, 119
  and ideology as distortion, 105–6, 107, 115
  influence on German sociologists, 36, 95, 102
  theory unrealistic in practice, 144–7

medical studies, 27, 29–31, 83, 86
  influence in sociology, 30–1, 86–90

Meerländer, Herr (factory owner), 32

Meier, Franz (school friend), 26

military service, 3, 20–1, 22–7
  effect on Elias's work, 86, 93
  see also war; World War One

minorities, 127–8
  see also Jews; outsiders

monopoly
  of power by state, 43–4, 141–2, 145–7

monopoly (*cont.*)
  theory of monopoly
    mechanism, 138–9, 149
Mörike, Eduard, 85
Mussolini, Benito, 61
mythology, as obscuring veil,
  36–8, 39–40
  see also ideology

national identity, 57
National Socialism, 41–2, 43,
  51–2, 103
  at Heidelberg, 99, 103
  dangers not foreseen, 38–9,
    41, 47
  and raid on sociology
    department, 48–9
nationalism
  lack of enthusiasm for, 16,
    18, 20–1
  as mythology, 37, 39
  in Weimar Republic, 129
nationality
  on feeling British, 62–3
  on feeling European, 74–5
  on feeling German, 10–11,
    16–21, 79–80, 121
Neustadt, Ilya (Leicester), 65,
  68

Oppenheimer, Franz
  (Heidelberg), 94
outsiders
  being one, 18–19, 66–7, 75
  Jews as, 19, 121–30

Paris, exile in, 49–51
patriotism, lack of, 17, 18,
  20–1
philosophy, studies in, 29–31,

  83, 86, 88, 91–3
poetry
  as answer to need for
    myths, 40
  interest in, 2, 14, 16
Poland, 5–6, 20, 23, 25
politics
  in Germany, 28–9, 43–9,
    98–9
  realistic attitude to, 39, 43–6,
    90–1
Popper, Karl, 66–7, 136
power
  concepts of, 141–5
  mistaken for freedom, 139
  state monopoly of, 43–4,
    145–7
psychoanalysis
  effect of personal, 64–5
  interest in group, 63
publications
  Greek anecdotes in *Berliner
    Illustrierte*, 33, 91
  essay on expulsion of
    Huguenots from France, 50
  essay on Kitsch style, 50
  The Civilizing Process, 52–6,
    61, 134
  What is Sociology?, 40, 141
  The Court Society, 55, 141
  The Society of Individuals, 64

railway journeys, significant
  memories of, 15–16, 23, 24
realism
  as goal, 36–8, 39–40, 43–6
  see also idealism
religion
  ideology having power of,
    148–51

Jewish, 122, 129
living without, 77–8
as mythology, 37–8
in primitive societies, 71
Rickert (Heidelberg), 95
Ries, Dr (French teacher), 84
Romania, 20
Russia
and the 'double bind', 148–51
experience and perception of,
19–20, 23

Scheidemann, Philipp, 28
Scheler (Heidelberg), 94
Schiller, Friedrich von, 18, 85
self-detachment, and concept of
figurational sociology,
133–41, 151
self-restraint
and absolutism, 59–60
in primitive societies, 70–1
and social interdependence,
140–1
Simmel, Georg, and German
sociology, 36, 94–5, 135
Snow, C. P., 62, 67
Social Democratic party,
Germany, 14, 27, 28, 42,
43–4
The Society of Individuals, 64
sociology
effect of grounding in other
disciplines, 30–1, 81–4,
86–90, 131–2
Elias's studies in, 34, 35–6,
83, 96
figurational, 130–51
German, 36, 94–5
influence of medical studies
on, 30–1, 86–90

narrowing professionalization
of, 81–2, 130–1
as study of long-term social
processes, 38, 101, 119–20,
131–2
Sombart, Werner (Heidelberg),
94, 110, 132
state
formation, 127–8, 134
and monopoly of power,
43–4, 141–2, 145–7
as servant of capitalism,
145–6
Stenzel, Julius (classics teacher),
84

Die Tat and right-wing sociology
group, 98–9
Tavistock Clinic, 63
Therapeutic Society, 63
Tönnies, Ferdinand
(Heidelberg), 94
Troeltsch (Heidelberg), 94–5
Turek, Ludwig (Paris), 49–50

United States, and the 'double
bind', 148–51

'validity', rejection of concept of,
34, 89, 91–2
violence
German propensity to, 41,
43–4
state monopoly of, 43–4,
141–2, 145–7
von Wiese, Leopold, 36, 110

war
emotional detachment
from, 16, 19, 20–1, 29

war (*cont.*)
  experience of service, 15–27, 87
  shock of, 26–7
  theory of 'the double bind', 22, 148–51
  see also military service; World War One; World War Two
Weber, Alfred, 1, 102–4, 109–20, 132
  and Elias's thesis on scientific thinking, 41, 98
  and his brother Max, 36, 94, 99–100, 114–15
  politics of, 39, 95, 99, 103
  possible *Habilitation* supervisor, 96, 98, 99
  rivalry with Mannheim, 34, 104, 109–20
Weber, Marianne (widow of Max), 36, 94, 96–8
Weber, Max, 35–6, 83, 94, 99–100, 132
  concept of power, 141–4
  Mannheim critical of,

114–15, 116
  relationship with wife, 97
Weimar Republic, 28–9, 36, 43, 129
  see also Germany
Wertheimer, Max (psychologist), 42
What is Sociology?, 40, 141
Wilhelm, Crown Prince, 61
Wilhelm II, Kaiser, 21, 28–9, 60–1, 90
  Elias's antipathy towards, 16–17, 19, 28–9
Wootton, Barbara (later Baroness Wootton), 81
work, attitude to, 3, 75, 78
World War One
  emotional uninvolvement in, 16, 19, 20–1, 29
  outbreak, 15–16
  stupidity of leaders, 21–2
World War Two, 62

Zentrum für interdisziplinäre Forschung (ZiF), Bielefeld, 1–2, 74

'Norbert Elias became an international celebrity late in life: this invaluable book now tells us where he came from. Not only does Elias explain his intellectual antecedents but, in one of his rare on-the-record ventures into personal reminiscence, we catch a glimpse of the young man Elias – in the Kaiser's Germany, in the Weimar era, and in exile.'

Stephen Mennell, University College Dublin

'In *Reflections on a Life* Elias successfully interweaves autobiography with sociological discussion in an accessible and always interesting way. The book is essential reading for anyone wanting to understand what it was that Elias *really* wrote and how he himself conceived of his work.'

Eric Dunning, University of Leicester

Once viewed as an outsider, Norbert Elias has come to be regarded as one of the key social thinkers of the twentieth century. His book *The Civilizing Process* has been acclaimed as a modern classic throughout the world.

Reflections on a Life includes a detailed interview with Elias in which he discusses different stages in his life and career: from his upbringing within a middle-class family to his experiences as a soldier during the First World War; from his student days in Heidelberg to the beginning of the Nazi period, when he emigrated firstly to France and then to England, where he taught for many years at the University of Leicester.

The second part of the book is an intellectual autobiography in which Elias discusses the connection between the development of his theories and his life experience.

Reflections on a Life will be essential reading for anyone who wishes to understand the work of one of the most original thinkers of our time.

Norbert Elias was Professor Emeritus at the University of Frankfurt until his death in 1990.

Cover illustration: Norbert Elias, 1984. Photo: Bert Nienhuis.

Cover design by Richard Boxall Design Associates
Printed in Great Britain

ISBN 0-7456-1383-7

Polity Press